Professional Correctness

Professional Correctness

LITERARY STUDIES AND POLITICAL CHANGE

Stanley Fish

Clarendon Press · Oxford
1995

Oxford University Press, Walton Street, Oxford OX2 6DP

Oxford New York
Athens Auckland Bangkok Bombay
Calcutta Cape Town Dar es Salaam Delhi
Florence Hong Kong Istanbul Karachi
Kuala Lumpur Madras Madrid Melbourne
Mexico City Nairobi Paris Singapore
Taipei Tokyo Toronto
and associated companies in
Berlin Ibadan

Oxford is a trade mark of Oxford University Press

Published in the United States
by Oxford University Press Inc., New York

British Library Cataloguing in Publication Data
Data available

Library of Congress Cataloging in Publication Data
Fish, Stanley Eugene.
Professional correctness: literary studies and political change /
Stanley Fish.
1. Criticism. 2. Political correctness in literature.
3. Literature—Political aspects. 4. Literature—Social aspects.
I. Title.
PN81.F57 1995 801'.95—dc20 95–19897
ISBN 0–19–812373–6

1 3 5 7 9 10 8 6 4 2

Set by Hope Services (Abingdon) Ltd.
Printed in Great Britain
on acid-free paper by
Bookcraft Ltd.
Midsomer Norton, Bath

This book is dedicated to L. Glenn Black, Christopher and Gillian Butler, Andrew Lockett, Helen Nicolaou, Joseph Raz, Vicki Reeve, Kim Scott Walwyn, and the many others who showed such kindness to two strangers in Oxford.

Preface

THIS book is a revised and expanded version of The Clarendon Lectures delivered at Oxford in the middle two weeks of May, 1993. I can say without reservation and with a great deal of nostalgia that this brief period was a highlight of my life in the academy, now approaching its thirty-fifth year. In revising, I have chosen to accentuate rather than remove traces of the lecture mode, and I have incorporated, wherever possible, the responses of those who heard the lectures and spoke or wrote to me in the intervals between them.

I owe a special debt of gratitude to friends and colleagues who read the manuscript and made many valuable suggestions. They are Homi Bhabha, Jonathan Crewe, Peter Goodrich, Howard Horwitz, William Kerrigan, Walter Benn Michaels, Richard Ohmann, Thomas Pfau, Stanley Stewart, and Hap Veeser.

In this list one name stands out for me. Howard Horwitz twice gifted me with marathon telephone conversations totalling perhaps thirty hours. In these conversations, Howard let no sentence stand until he had imagined and warned against the misapprehensions it might provoke unrevised. I don't know whether this is friendship, but it will do.

It has been pointed out by Homi Bhabha, Peter Goodrich, and Hap Veeser (personal communication), that my own performance in these lectures might be seen to contradict their thesis, since I, myself, 'stand astride disciplines and speak to a public sphere' (Goodrich).

To this I would say, one does not range across disciplines for no reason, and the reasons that lead one to range will always be task specific; therefore, the materials one quarries while ranging will be seen and configured through the lens of that task. This kind of ranging, in short, does not mark a departure from a disciplinary focus, but a sharpening of it. This is quite a different thing from the interdisciplinarity against which I argue in this book; the difference lies in the claims of that more ambitious project—to blur the boundaries between academic subjects or between the academy and the world, to enlarge the mind, to loosen the constraints imposed by 'parochial' disciplines. It is these claims that I reject, but my rejection of them does not deprive me of the resources of other disciplines when I sit down to do a particular job of work. In this book, that job (as I assign it to myself) is a consideration of the relationship between academic labours and political change. In the course of undertaking that consideration, I look at this discipline and at that one, sometimes contrasting them, sometimes aligning them, but always viewing them from the perspective of the questions with which I begin. Thus I do not *do* history or legal theory or philosophy in these pages; rather, I make reference to the internal workings of these disciplines when I think that such a reference will help me to clarify a distinction or respond to an anticipated objection. The one moment when the task-specific focus of my performance is relaxed occurs in Lecture V when my analysis of a line from *Paradise Lost* ceases being an example of something and is pursued for its own sake. At that moment I am not enriching my central thesis, or deepening it; I am abandoning it, doing literary criticism rather than talking about doing literary criticism.

Another early reader of these pages wondered about the relationship between my strong defence of disciplinary integrity and the thesis of social constructionism which seems such a threat to integrity of any kind. In fact, the thesis of social constructionism is a threat to nothing; or, rather, it is a threat only if it is asserted weakly. That is, the thesis of social constructionism can do genuine work only if it is limited, a thesis about some things but not about everything; only if it is a thesis about some things, does it enable a distinction between that which is socially constructed and that which is not. Armed with that distinction, one could then say about some discipline that it was more or less firmly grounded than some other. But if *everything* is socially constructed, the fact of a particular thing being socially constructed is not a fact you can do anything with. It won't help you to distinguish that socially constructed thing from all the other socially constructed things.

This does not mean that there are no differences to be noted between objects, activities, and structures, only that the differences cannot be marked by the presence, absence, or degree of social constructedness. Since, for example, history and literary studies are both social constructions, the fact of social constructedness (which they share) will not be a way of distinguishing between them, and in search of the appropriate distinctions you will be turned back to the 'immanent intelligibility' each displays in its equally (but differently) socially constructed form; that is, you will be turned back to the everyday routines, disciplinary features, canonical problems, and established authorities that were obvious and perspicuous for you before you went down the (dead-end) road of social constructionism. Although it may seem paradoxical at first, the conclusion is unavoidable: the larger the asserted scope of social constructedness, the less it matters.

There are in general two wrong uses to which the thesis of social constructedness has been put. Sometimes it is used as a critique: 'aha, your agenda or project is socially constructed!'. But it can hardly be a criticism of something that it is socially constructed if everything is. At other times, it is said that once you see that something is socially constructed you are better able to revise it. But the impulse to revise has been experienced and acted upon long before social constructionism was ever thought up; and, moreover, those who have been persuaded to the social constructedness thesis are in no better position to revise than anyone else since the work of revision isn't furthered a whit by declaring it to be possible. The real work remains and will occur within the parameters, and in relation to the in-place machinery, of particular disciplines; the real work cannot be done or even begun by simply *announcing* the thesis of social constructedness.

My position on social constructionism is what distinguishes me from both sides of the debate about disciplines and disciplinary integrity. Most people who defend disciplines and their boundaries believe that in order to do so they must attack post-structuralist and post-modernist thought, and attack especially the notion that disciplines, like everything else, are socially constructed. Most post-modernists and post-structuralists, on the other hand, assume that the epistemology to which they have been persuaded and especially the anti-essentialism of that epistemology, commits them to denying the reality and efficacy of disciplinary boundaries. I assert, and assert without contradiction, that post-modernist accounts of how disciplines come into being are correct, but that such accounts, rather than telling us that disciplines are unreal tell us just how disciplines came to be as real and as productive as they are.

I would like to provide this book with two directions for the user. 1. Do not read it as evidence that I have changed my mind or my politics. 2. Do not read it as a repudiation of cultural studies, black studies, feminist studies, gay and lesbian studies, and other forms of activity that have reinvigorated the literary scene. The argument that unfolds here is absolutely continuous with arguments I have made since the late 1970s, and my support for non-traditional scholarship in the humanities is as strong as it ever was and extends to the work of many I criticize in these pages. What I question is not their accomplishments, which are many, but the claims that sometimes accompany those accomplishments, claims which are in my view uncashable. Nothing I say here should be construed as support for the neo-conservative assault on the humanities, an assault made up of equal parts of ignorance and malice. Of course I cannot prevent misreadings or the misappropriations they might enable, but I can certainly label them as such in advance.

My argument first began to take form in 1990 when I was

invited to give a seminar at the Folger Library. My Folger notes were then expanded into a pilot manuscript in the spring of 1992 when I was privileged to be a Fellow of the National Humanities Center in Research Park, North Carolina. Final revisions were completed in the course of my residence at the Center for Ideas and Society at the University of California at Riverside in the winter and spring of 1995. Along the way I was the beneficiary of the efforts and dedication of a marvelous staff, including Miriam Angress, Katie Courtland, Lisa Haarlander, Jan Martuscelli, Susan Ryman, and Anne Wills.

Contents

═══

===

Yet Once More

TO the ears of many in this audience, the lectures I am about to give will sound retrograde and reactionary because they go against the grain of much that has been said in recent years about literary and cultural studies. Specifically, I shall be questioning the possibility of transforming literary study so that it is more immediately engaged with the political issues that are today so urgent: issues of oppression, racism, terrorism, violence against women and homosexuals, cultural imperialism, and so on. It is not so much that literary critics have nothing to say about these issues, but that so long as they say it *as* literary critics no one but a few of their friends will be listening, and, conversely, if they say it in ways unrelated to the practices of literary criticism, and thereby manage to give it a political effectiveness, they will no longer be literary critics, although they will still be something and we may regard the something they will then be as more valuable.

The literary critic as I imagine him is anything but an organic intellectual in the Gramscian sense; instead he is a specialist, defined and limited by the traditions of his craft, and it is a condition of his labours, at least as they are exerted in the United States, that he remain distanced from any effort to work changes in the structure of society. It is not that society's structure is unalterable or that there could never come a day when the words of a literary critic will resound in the halls of congress; it is just that I do not see that day coming soon and I do not think that anything you or I could do will bring it closer. Samuel Goldwyn once said in response to someone who asked him why his movies were not more concerned with important social issues, 'If I wanted to send a message, I'd use Western Union.' I say, if you want to send a message that will be heard beyond the academy, get out of it. Or, if I may adapt a patriotic slogan, 'the academy—love it or leave it'.

I am aware of course that simply to utter such pronouncements is to invite a barrage of objections—who are you to say? isn't this a return to the discredited notion of the mandarin intellectual? aren't you presenting one more brief for the status quo?—and in the course of writing and revising these lectures I have tried to anticipate those objections and to reply to them. I have used as a heuristic device someone I thought of as The Cultural Critic, and at every point I have asked myself, 'What would The Cultural Critic say? Providence always provides, and in this case Providence provided a book by Alan Sinfield entitled *Faultlines: Cultural Materialism and the Politics of Dissident Reading* (Berkeley, Los Angeles, 1992). In that book Sinfield has some harsh things to say about me, although not so harsh as the things said recently by Christopher Norris, who at times seems to hold me (along with Richard Rorty, Baudrillard, and Lyotard) responsible for the Gulf War. Sinfield says that I 'totalize'—a major crime in his lexicon, perhaps equivalent to serial murder; that I employ a 'bullying tone'—well, he has a point there; that I desire to entrap 'understanding within a closed system'; and that I am 'complacent' in contrast to the new historicists who have the good grace to be *'anxious about* entrapment' (288–90). I would say instead that anxiety about entrapment is the new historicist's version of complacency; anxiety, of a particularly self-righteous kind, is what they do for a living. At any rate the difference between me and Sinfield is helpfully stark and it can be measured by one of his pronouncements: 'Literary criticism tells its own stories. It is, in effect, a subculture, asserting its own distinctive criteria of plausibility' (51). I couldn't agree more; in fact the word

'distinctive' will play a large part in my argument and the ways of
plausibility—or, as I put it, of 'immanent intelligibility'—are my
subject. Sinfield, however, regards the plausibility of literary criticism as a sham and a lure; 'coherence', he announces, 'is a
chimera'; it obscures the multiform nature of what it tries to
domesticate and it is often in complicity with the most 'regressive
aspects of our cultural formation' (51). My view of coherence,
plausibility, and distinctiveness is more benign; together they
underwrite the culture in which I am privileged to work (and
indeed any culture in which anyone could work), and in what follows I trace out the lineaments of that culture without apologiz-
ing for it.

I shall begin by offering an example of the kind of story the literary culture characteristically tells, and I have chosen as my
vehicle the first three words of Milton's *Lycidas*. What follows is
an analysis that would seem familiar and even ordinary to literary actors in general and Miltonists in particular. The analysis is
thus a sample piece of work rather than the work I would do if I
were writing an essay for submission to *Milton Studies*. In that
essay, which I will now *not* write, I would focus on the image of a
body weltering to the parching wind, and thereby becoming
parchment, and I would observe that such a body/surface is available for inscription by forces indifferent to its previous history. I
would then link this observation to the tropes of writing on
water, walking on water, and drowning in water, all of which, I
would say, are refractions of Milton's fear of strong women who
will either overwhelm you, abandon you, or tear you to pieces
and send your head down the stream toward the Lesbian shore.

However, you're not going to hear any of that; rather, you will
hear a reading of the poem that assigns it meanings most workers in the field would find (relatively) uncontroversial. I will be
committed to that reading only as an example of the present state
of the art, an example that will allow me to pose some general
questions about the art and about the conditions of its intelligibility. The difference between the two analyses, the one I shall

[3]

withhold and the one I shall elaborate, is the difference between the answers to two (different) questions: (1) what reading of *Lycidas* do I believe to be true?, and (2) what reading of *Lycidas* will best serve the purpose of the present study? The point may seem laboured or uninteresting, but I ask you to keep it in mind and promise you that in time it will connect up with some larger issues.

The first three words of Milton's *Lycidas* are 'Yet once more', and any reading of the poem must begin with those words. But how does one begin? Is 'Yet' to be read as 'Despite' and therefore as referring to a previously noted reluctance to act that has now been overcome? 'Forget what I've just been saying; we're going to do it again' '*Yet*, once more'. Or is this the 'yet' of exasperation, introducing a repetition whose occurrence is regretted even as it is announced? Is the 'once-moreness' of the yet-to-be described action infused with a profound and disappointed weariness: 'My God, must we do this *again*?' 'Yet once *more*?' To choose between these readings (and they of course are not the only possible ones) is to choose between alternative imaginings of the situation from which the words issue, where 'situation' is an inadequate short-hand for such matters as the identity of the speaker—what kind of person is he? where has he been? where is he going?; the nature of his project—what is he trying to do?; the occasion of its performance—what has moved him to do it?

It might seem that these and related questions are conveniently answered by the headnote that stands between the title and the first line:

In this Monody the author bewails a learned Friend, unfortunately drown'd in his Passage from *Chester* on the *Irish* Seas, 1637. And by occasion foretels the ruine of our corrupted Clergy, then in their height.

But rather than narrowing interpretive options, the headnote proliferates them, if only because of its own publishing history. When the poem first appeared in 1638 there was no headnote, although a manuscript dated November 1637 includes the first sentence. The second sentence, 'And by occasion foretels the ruine of our corrupted Clergy, then in their height', was added in 1645 when the author published a volume entitled *Poems of Mr. John Milton*. These few facts raise a distressing number of questions. If the first half of the headnote was written before the 1638 publication, why was it omitted?

One answer might be that since the poem was printed along with other tributes to the 'unfortunately drown'd' learned friend in a memorial collection entitled *Justa Edovardo King*, there was no need for an identification of its occasion. If this common-sense explanation were taken seriously it would demand a reading of the poem in the context of its companion pieces. We would be obliged to consider it not as a free-standing artefact produced by a single consciousness, but as a component in an ensemble effort. This, however, would have the problematic effect of suggesting that the 1645 version, differently situated, was a different poem, for instead of offering itself as one of a number of responses to a distressing fact—the death of a mutual friend—the poem would offer itself as evidence of the talent of a newly emerged poet. It would then be read in the context of the other productions in the same volume, which would include poems that find Milton worrying obsessively about the late maturing of his talent ('How soon hath time the subtle thief of youth, | Stol'n on his wing my three and twentieth year') and wondering whether he is making the best possible use of his gifts. These same concerns are expressed often in the prose writings of this period where, typically, they take the form of a complaint by the poet that he has been interrupted in his studies and forced to take on a task he would rather have declined. He has been compelled, he says in *The Reason of Church Government*, to 'write . . . out of mine own season, when I have neither yet compleated to my minde the full circle of my private studies' (*The Complete Prose Works of John Milton*, ed. Don Wolfe *et al.*, New Haven, 1953, i. 807). With passages like this in mind, *Lycidas*, with its elaborate metaphor of a

'season due' that has not been allowed to mature, will seem but
one more such interruption: 'Yet once more'. Yet once more I have
been plucked from the 'still time' of contemplation and thrust
willy-nilly into the world of chance and mischance.

So far we have been proceeding (if that is the word, for after all
we are still stuck on the poem's opening phrase) by looking back-
ward to the possible antecedents of this moment of utterance; if
we now go only slightly forward to the poem's next phrase, we
find still further complications in the shape of additional interpretive alternatives: 'Yet once more, O ye laurels'. Note first the
oddness of the address; one does not usually talk to trees. Of
course, one does talk to trees and to all manner of other things in
poems, and one is obligated to talk to trees in poems that belong
to the category of *pastoral*. The generic identification is made in
a note by Thomas Warton in 1791 when he observes that 'by
plucking the berries and the leaves of the laurel, myrtle and ivy,
[Milton] might intend to point out the pastoral or rural turn of
his poem' (*Poems upon Several Occasions, English, Italian, and Latin
with Translations, by John Milton*, ed. Thomas Warton, 2nd edn.,
1791, 2). But this can only be pointed out to a reader who already
knows it, who already knows (among other things) that there is a
genre called pastoral and that one of its conventions is an address
to nature and natural processes. When I say 'knows' I don't mean
that the reader holds in reserve, and then applies, knowledge in
order to give shape to a landscape that is as yet undifferentiated;
rather it is within the requisite knowledge that the reader proceeds, and he quite literally sees the landscape into shape, filling
in its details not after a first, uninterpretive reading but in the
course of a first (not really the first since it is motored by all the
previous readings that make it possible if not inevitable) reading.
The direction of inference in Warton's observation (despite the
footnote which suggests a process more inductive) is neither
from a knowledge of the genre to a specification of the laurel's
significance, nor from a noting of the laurel's significance to a
specification of the genre; indeed it is not an inference he makes

at all, but an (involuntary) act of recognition (*re*-cognition) in which the genre and the significance of particular details come into view immediately and simultaneously.

That act occurs as early as the taking in of the poem's title, for among the things that a reader like Warton knows is that 'Lycidas' and like names are commonly found in poems that depict an idealized shepherd life that is used as a backdrop or frame within which a poet meditates on a range of issues including (the list is not exhaustive) agricultural policies, urban decay, civic responsibility, ecclesiastical corruption, military ambitions, economics, the pains of love, and the place of poetry in a world hostile to its existence. This last is particularly important because it marks the genre as a self-reflexive one. Moreover, it has been self-reflexive from the beginning, or rather, since its *non*-beginning. Theocritus, the 'first' pastoral poet, was not situated in a rural scene from which his successors were progressively more removed; he was himself already removed; a participant in the 'decadent' literary life of third-century Alexandria, his representation of an idyllic pastoral landscape is at best a remembered re-creation of a childhood in Sicily, a re-creation that breathes *loss* from its very first word. It is a paradox (and strength) of the genre that its preferred values are in a state of disintegration long before they are celebrated. The valorization of the 'natural' and simple life of shepherds and shepherdesses is made in the context of a pervasive nostalgia, which means that the very notion of 'the natural' is a construction of high artifice, a point emphasized by George Puttenham in 1589 when he declared that the intention of pastoral poetry is not to 'represent the rusticall manner . . . but under the vaile of homely persons . . . to insinuate and glaunce at greater matters' (*The Arte of English Poesy*, London, 1589, 55).

What this means is that everyone who writes in the genre does so with a sense of belatedness, of having missed the beauty and equanimity of a form of life that can be invoked only after the fact of its passing. The poet who would add his voice to a long line of lamenting predecessors knows that he takes up a task (of sounding the 'oaten' note) only in order to re-experience its failure, *yet once more*. In another tradition, however—a tradition also formative of a practised reader's consciousness—'yet once more' is strongly associated with a force that turns temporal failure into eternal success. The force is, quite simply, the force of God, whose apocalyptic promise (or is it a threat?) is reported by Paul in his Epistle to the Hebrews: 'Yet once more I shake not the earth only but also heaven.' Almost as if he were a literary critic, Paul immediately supplies the gloss: 'this word, Yet once more, signifieth the removing of those things that are shaken, as of things that are made, that those things which cannot be shaken may remain. Wherefore, receiving a kingdom which cannot be moved, let us have grace, by which we may serve God acceptably with reverence and godly fear: For our God is a consuming fire' (Heb. 12: 26–9). That is, if I may gloss Paul's gloss (notice how we become ever more deeply embedded in the layered history of hermeneutics), the godly 'Yet once more' announces the firm and everlasting foundation that underlies a world of *apparent* contingency announced by the secular 'Yet once more'. The 'shaking' men and women experience from the vantage-point of their limited perspective is from God's perspective a 'shaking down', at the end of which will remain only those things that abide. But since no one of us inhabits God's perspective, the permanence that underwrites and finally mitigates temporal instability is not something we can apprehend, and, as Paul explains elsewhere (notably in the eleventh chapter of Hebrews), we must therefore take it on faith, defined famously as 'the substance of things hoped for, the evidence of things not seen'.

It would seem, then, incumbent on us to hear two distinctive notes or voices in the opening words of Milton's poem: the weary voice of the beleaguered mortal who has just experienced what seems to him to be a cataclysmic shaking (the early and apparently senseless death of a good and talented man) and the confident voice of a deity who proclaims a truth that can be neither questioned nor verified (it is, by definition, its own evidence).

Not coincidentally, these two voices correspond to the two strains of the pastoral in which Milton is necessarily (he has no choice) participating: the historically prior strain of the classical pastoral as established, in a kind of godly fiat, by Theocritus, and the biblical pastoral which takes its cue from Christ's declaration 'I am the good shepherd; the good shepherd giveth his life for the sheep' (John 10: 11). The intersection of these two strains creates a double discourse in which landscapes and the values associated with them are systematically opposed. On one hand an idyllic landscape imagined as a safe (if precarious) retreat from the pressures of 'modern' life, especially the life of the city; on the other a harsh and forbidding landscape whose central figure is not an immature, lovestruck shepherd, but an older and much burdened minister of the gospel who must give aid and comfort to a (human) flock beset with every trouble against which one might take arms.

The contrast is between the pastoral of ease or *otium* and the pastoral of care or moral responsibility, and it is a contrast that itself becomes a commonplace theme in medieval and Renaissance instances of the genre. Spenser's *February Eclogue*, for example, is structured as a dialogue between the two traditions as represented by the frivolous Cuddie and the oh-so-serious Thenot, who lectures his younger compatriot thus:

> Selfe have I worne out thrise threttie yeares,
> Some in much joy, many in many teares:
> Yet never complained of cold nor heate,
> of Sommers flame, nor of Winters threate,
> Ne ever was to fortune foeman,
> But gently tooke, that ungently came.
> And ever my flocke was my chief care,
> Winter or Sommer they mought well fare.   (17–23)

In the *May Eclogue* the same opposition is continued by two other shepherds, Palinode and Piers (obviously intended to recall Langland's Piers the Ploughman), who looks beyond the present moment of pain and care to a day of final judgement:

[9]

Thilke same bene shepeheards for the Devils stedde,
That playen, while their flockes be unfedde . . .
I muse what account both these will make . . .
When great *Pan* account of shepeherdes shall aske.

(43–4, 51, 54)

Thenot's forward-looking vision rebukes the *carpe diem* sentiments expressed by Palinode (shepherds should 'Reapen the
fruite . . . | The while they here liven, at ease and leasure') and
points to a salient difference between the two pastoral strains, the
one with its emphasis on the moment-to-moment passing of carnal time, the other with at least one eye (and that the clear-
sighted eye) on the treasure that *already* awaits those who endure
this life in the hope ('the substance of things hoped for') of
another in eschatological time. It is a prime thesis of the biblical
pastoral that carnal time is finally unreal, that, as Milton puts it in
another poem, time's primary task is to cannibalize itself:

Fly envious Time . . .
And glut thyself with what thy womb devours,
Which is no more than that what is false and vain,
And merely mortal dross.

(*On Time*, 1, 4–6)

When this process is completed,

Then all this earthly grossness quit,
Attir'd with stars, we shall forever sit,
Triumphing over death and chance and thee, O Time.

(20–22)

This view of time is also a view of both the location and production of *meaning*. In the world of carnal or secular time meaning lies waiting at the end of a sequence; it emerges, quite
literally, only in the 'fulness of time'. In the Christian vision,
sequence is not productive of meaning, but rather marks out
spaces (like the tick-tock of a metronome) in which an already
full meaning, the meaning of Christ's redemptive act, is available

to those who have the eyes to apprehend it; those, that is, for whom the evidence need *not* be seen. In this vision time is reversible, as it is for the God of *Paradise Lost*, who 'from his prospect high | . . . past, present future . . . beholds' (III. 78–9). Moreover, since the spaces of time are filled always by the same meaning, individual agency is finally unimportant: in the eyes or ears of the faithful, God's message is manifest no matter who speaks. Intention is not a property of limited consciousnesses but of the spirit that makes of them an involuntary vehicle. For centuries Virgil's fourth eclogue, known as the messianic eclogue, was read as a prophecy of the birth of Christ, a reading that would be dismissed as anachronistic by a post-Enlightenment mind, but one that would seem quite appropriate and even inevitable to a mind schooled in the ways of interpretation by St Augustine's *On Christian Doctrine* and accustomed to thinking of Dante's *Divine Comedy*, graced by a Christianized Virgil, as a sacred text.

Augustine himself builds on an interpretive strategy already present in the epistles of Paul. It is called typology and it emerged first as a way of reading events chronicled in the Old Testament as prefigurations, or 'shadows', of events in the life of Christ. In typological interpretations the actions of men and nations derive their significance not only from the conditions of their historical production, but from a master significance, Christ's work of incarnation and redemption, which is 'before' history, in the sense of already having occurred in eternity, and yet is nevertheless the content of history in that every apparently discrete action at once reflects and anticipates it. In the course of the centuries strict typological interpretation is relaxed and the method is extended to the lives and deeds of contemporary agents, both individual and collective, and in the seventeenth century Puritans of Milton's temper routinely saw themselves as re-enacting the Old Testament 'remnant', those few faithful who followed the call of God and, led by Moses (a type of Christ), struck out for the Promised Land, for Canaan, the type of Paradise and eternal life.

It is not too much to say that from the typological perspective each moment is equivalent to all others, offering the same challenge, the challenge of affirming God's promise in the face of the contrary evidence often thrown up by 'the world', and holding out the same reward, salvation and reunion with divinity, to those who hold fast; each moment in short is a repetition of the same, and therefore an instance of a meaning that is proclaimed *yet once more*.

It is not proclaimed by anyone in particular, although anyone at all can be its vehicle. That is why Milton is able to present himself in the headnote to *Lycidas* as a non-privileged reader of his own poem, or rather, of what has turned out to be *not* his own poem. When he says 'And by occasion foretels the ruine of our corrupted Clergy, then in their height' he is not so much claiming the power of prophecy (although Virgilian precedent—and Milton self-consciously modelled his career on Virgil's—would have authorized him to do so) as he is finding (with the delight of the believer) meanings that he did not himself intend. In *The Reason of Church Government*, written in 1642, he had declared, 'When God commands to take the trumpet, and blow a dolorous and jarring blast, it lies not in man's will what he shall say, or what he shall conceal' (*Complete Prose Works*, i. 803). Now, in 1645 he discovers just how jarring was the blast he unwittingly blew in 1637 when he thought he was simply lamenting the death of a friend and a loss to the Church but was in fact (God's fact, God's intention) foretelling, with an authority for which he was not responsible, the fall of Bishop Laud and of the entire institution of prelacy. Read this way, the headnote instructs us in how to read the poem's first three words, not as the anguished cry of a belated and ineffectual singer, as would be the case were the context limited to the classical strain inaugurated by Theocritus, but as the confident affirmation by a voice that will always make itself heard no matter how weak or transitory its vessel. In effect, by making this reading of his poem available—that is, by reporting in the headnote, with no hint of resentment, that this poem was commandeered 'by occasion' by a power greater than his—Milton acknowledges and accepts his radical dependency, accepts and acknowledges his 'yet-once-moreness'.

I could go on for ever in this vein—I haven't been a Miltonist these thirty years for nothing—adding to the contexts I have already introduced the context of Italian verse forms, the context of the myth of Orpheus, even the context of Jungian archetypes; but enough has been done, I trust, to support my point, which is not that *Lycidas* is complex, but that *Lycidas* is a poem. I would not deny *Lycidas* the attribute of complexity; I merely assert that the compliment is tautological. Simply to *be* a poem, that is, to have been categorized in that way rather than as a political pamphlet or a sermon, is to have been credited with linguistic and semantic density, even in advance of its discovery. Moreover, that discovery, once the categorization has been granted, is *assured* not in its details (which can vary in all the ways we have already seen) but in a general shape that will be filled out by the interpretive activities generated by the knowledge (quite literally *working* knowledge) that it is a poem one is interpreting.

Linguistic and semantic density is not something poems announce, but something that readers actualize by paying to texts labelled poetic a kind of attention they would not pay to texts not so labelled. Were 'Yet once more' the first three words of a parliamentary speech or an address by a general to his troops, the addressees would not be hearing them as they hear them when they are the first three words of *Lycidas*; or, and this is to make the same point from the other direction, were the parliamentarians or the infantrymen to ring the interpretive changes I have rung in the preceding paragraphs, they would be understood (and understand themselves) to be acting in ways inappropriate to the community of which they were, at that moment, members. It is not that it couldn't be done (in fact it can *always* be done), but that doing it—treating a political speech or a hortatory appeal as a poem—would be recognized by everyone concerned, including the doers, as play of a kind that was not to the institutional point and, indeed, flouted it.

When I use words like 'institution' or 'community' I refer not to a collection of independent individuals who, in a moment of deliberation, *choose* to employ certain interpretive strategies, but rather to a set of practices that are defining of an enterprise and fill the consciousnesses of the enterprise's members. Those members include the authors and speakers as well as their interpreters. Indeed they are *all* interpreters: when Milton puts pen to paper he no less than those in his intended audience is a reader of his own action. That is, as he begins, he thinks of himself, or, to be more precise, he conceives of himself, as a worker in a long-established field; and as such a worker he knows what gestures are available to him and the extent to which he is obliged to perform them, and the meaning they will have for those who are situated as he is, in the same field. If one understands the relationship between writers and their readers in this way, not as a relationship between agents with differing tasks and objectives but as one between agents engaged in the mutual performance of a single task, my assertion a moment ago that complexity is something that readers actualize will seem less disturbing than it perhaps was when it could be heard as an assertion of an interpretive will to power. Readers who perform in the ways I have been describing—in ways I have been exemplifying—do not ride roughshod over an author's intention; rather they *match* it by going about their business at once constrained and enabled by the same history that burdens and energizes those whom they read. Like all interpreters they are engaged in the project of determining intention, of asking 'What does he or she or they or it *mean*?', but that determination itself depends on the assumption (not self-consciously arrived at but deployed in some sense involuntarily) of an intention, the intention, imputed to the author and directive of the reader's activities, of making a *poem*.

Another way to put this is to say that both readers and interpreters begin (exactly the wrong word) *in medias res*; they go about their business not in order to discover its point, but already in possession of and possessed by its point. They ask questions and give answers—not, however, any old questions and answers, but questions and answers of the kind they know in advance to be relevant. In a sense they could not even ask the questions if they did not already know the answers to questions deeper than the ones they are explicitly asking. My own practice to this point can serve as an example. In the preceding pages I have been asking questions about the interpretation of literary texts, but I have been guided, unselfconsciously, by my pre-assumed understanding of what kind of thing literary interpretation *is*, an understanding which itself rests on a (tacit) understanding of what kind of thing literature is. The ease with which I multiplied interpretive alternatives in the supposed service of posing a question— what is literary interpretation?—is an answer to it. That is, I knew (not in a way that guided my practice, but in a way that constituted its intelligibility for me and for my peers) that literary texts are polysemous, that they are multivoiced, that they often assert *A* and not-*A* simultaneously and that they can be read from right to left as well as from left to right.

It was this knowledge that led me to put an interpretive *pressure* on the first three words of *Lycidas* that would have been inappropriate (and, presumably, unrewarding, although this is a matter less straightforward than it might seem) in relation to a text that was not identified as literary. It might have appeared that I was telling you what you have to know before you can read *Lycidas*, but in fact I was telling you what you have to know in order even to ask what you have to know before you can read *Lycidas*. Or, rather, I was not *telling* you what you have to know in order even to ask what you have to know before you can read *Lycidas*; I was *showing* you, offering myself as an example, much as a tennis coach does when he says to a pupil, 'Do it like this'. Indeed, I could not have told you, if I had tried, what you have to know in order even to ask what you have to know before you can read *Lycidas*, for the words that I would have used and the directions I might have given would have been intelligible only within the knowledge they purport to convey.

Where does that knowledge—which I wasn't offering discursively but exemplifying, which is, in some sense, too deep for words—come from? Surely not from the text, which acquires its generic shape and particular details only in the light of that knowledge. It comes, if it 'comes' from anywhere, from the fact of my embeddedness (almost embodiment) in a field of practice that marks its members with signs that are immediately perspicuous to one another. These signs are not visible on the surface; rather they emerge when a member is offered a piece of behaviour by a non-member—by an outsider—and responds (the response may be nothing more than a discreet nod to another member) by saying ('saying', strictly speaking, isn't required; a change in expression caught and read by another member will suffice) 'That's not the kind of thing we do around here'. It would not be to the point to ask what exactly 'the kind of thing we do here' is, because it is known precisely in the way suggested by the statement, not as a discrete item, but in contrast with the kind of thing done by members of other enterprises (history, sociology, statistics). As Bruce Robbins has put it, 'professionalism in any one discipline is inseparable from, and indeed, defined by, the relations *among* disciplines' (*Secular Vocations: Intellectuals, Professionalism, Culture*, London, 1993, 115). The content of 'kind of thing we do here' is differential; it comes into view against a background of the practices it is *not*; and it must 'show' in that way—as something we, not others, do—because if it did not it could not sustain a challenge to its usefulness.

John Crowe Ransom made the point a long time ago when he found it 'atrocious' for an English department 'to abdicate its own self-respecting identity' by failing to establish and defend 'the peculiar constitution and structure of its product'. English, he thundered, 'might almost as well announce that it does not regard itself as entirely autonomous, but as a branch of the department of history, with the option of declaring itself occasionally a branch of the department of ethics' ('Criticism, Inc.', in *The World's Body*, Port Washington, NY, 1964, 335). Ransom would seem here to be prophetic in foreseeing the eagerness of many literary academics to do just that in the name of the new historicism and of political criticism, and I shall have much to say about the unwisdom of these two projects. For the moment, however, I am content simply to register my agreement with Ransom's insistence that it is a requirement for the respectability of an enterprise that it be, or at least be able to present itself as, *distinctive*.

Distinctiveness: Its Achievement and Its Costs

B Y 'distinctive' I mean nothing more or less than 'must be itself and not some other thing'. Note that this understanding of distinctiveness does not imply an endorsement of any of the shapes it might take. The fact that an enterprise acquires an identity by winning a space at the table of enterprises does not determine the specific features of that identity. Within the space that has been secured, all questions, including questions touching on basic concepts, remain open. Nor are the boundaries between enterprises fixed and impermeable; negotiations on the borders go on continually, and at times border skirmishes can turn into large-scale territorial disputes in which the right of an enterprise to the space it has long occupied is hotly contested. At those times internal debates will focus on fundamental issues of self-definition, and when the debates are concluded, or, rather, put temporarily to rest, the internal map of the enterprise will have been significantly altered, and the content of 'the kind of thing we do around here' will have changed.

What will not have changed, however—unless the enterprise is bent on suicide—is the fact that a certain set of activities is recognized as appropriate to *this* field. The enterprise will still present itself, both to the outside world and to its members, as uniquely qualified to perform a specific task. An enterprise that can make good on that claim will in an important way be autonomous, not autonomous in the sense of having no affiliations with or debts to other enterprises (that would be an impossible requirement, which, if met, would result in a practice wholly lacking in interest and human intelligibility), but autonomous in the sense of having primary responsibility for doing a job the society wants done.

In order to fill out this sense of autonomy or distinctiveness I want to step away, for a moment, from literary criticism, and turn to the field of law and to an argument made recently by a legal theorist whose question is not 'What is literary interpretation?' but 'What is the law of torts?' In an essay entitled 'Legal Formalism: On the Immanent Rationality of Law' (*Yale Law Journal*, 97/6, May 1988), Ernest J. Weinrib begins his answer to the question by declaring that

When we seek the intelligibility of something, we want to know *what* that something is. The search for 'whatness' presupposes that something is a *this* and not a *that*, that it has, in other words a determinate content. That content is determinate because it sets the matter apart from other matters, and prevents it from falling back into the chaos of unintelligible indeterminacy that its identification as a something denies. (958)

It follows then, says Weinrib, that 'Nothing is more senseless than to attempt to understand law from a vantage point extrinsic to it' (953), on the reasoning that any such attempt would yield an understanding of that 'extrinsic vantage point' (whatever it may be) and not of law. Unfortunately, Weinrib laments, just such attempts make up the bulk of legal scholarship today:

Implicit in contemporary scholarship is the idea that the law embodies or should embody some goal (e.g. wealth maximization, market deterrence, liberty, utility, solidarity) that can be specified apart from the law and can serve as the standard by which law is to be assessed. Thus law is regarded as an instrument for forwarding some independently desirable purpose given to it from the outside. (955)

Taking as a particularly seductive instance of the tendency he deplores the inclination of some jurists to defer to the findings of science, Weinrib strongly 'rejects the premise that our notion of legal understanding must follow in the ruts of scientific explanation' (964). Rather, legal understanding is an 'immanent' (internal) affair, and 'legal phenomena' will come into view only under the pressure of a legal analysis; otherwise they would not be *legal* phenomena but something else. An 'immanent understanding' is on this reasoning more basic than any that might be yielded by science since for legal purposes 'law is more perspicuous'—more revealing of what is going on—'than nature' and therefore 'it is a mistake to burden law with conclusions drawn from the scientist's external—and therefore less secure—mode of recognition' (964).

'Immanent understanding', as Weinrib conceives it, is not to be apprehended by itemizing features of the internal landscape, but by grasping the coherent set of purposes that confer value and significance and even shape on those features. It is that set of purposes, when they inform an insider's perception, that is responsible for his sense of what is and is not 'intuitively plausible' in the consideration of any legal problem. When a legal practitioner listens to a client's story, she listens with *legal* ears and what she hears is quite different in its emphases from what the client hears when he tells his sad tale. The client may stress a moment or action that appears to him to be defining of his cause only to hear the lawyer say that it is not something that can be brought under categories with which and within which the law thinks. (Actually she is saying that *she* cannot bring together his sense of distress and the currently authorized ways of 'legal talking'; there may be some other practitioner who could manage the feat, and in the event of which the criterion of 'intuitive plausibility' would not have been abandoned but refashioned.) 'A datum is legally significant,' Weinrib explains, 'not as a particular added to an aggregate of particulars, but as the instantiation of a category that can coherently combine with other legal categories' (976). The question one asks, then, of any particular for which significance is claimed is, does it cohere with other

[21]

particulars already rendered significant because of their relationship to accepted legal categories and ways of talking? If the answer is affirmative or can, in the process of discussion and elaboration, be *made* affirmative, the introduction of the particular will have been justified.

What this means is that justification—the process by which a move in the game is declared valid—is always internal and is never a matter of looking for confirmation to something outside the law's immanent intelligibility. The client who complains that his experience of an event has not been accommodated by the law's rewriting of it will remain unhappy because 'the crucial consideration is not what happened, but how one is to understand the justificatory structure that is latent in the legal arrangements that might deal with what happened' (985). Weinrib concedes that this account of justification renders it circular, since it 'does not strive for any standpoint beyond the law, the most it can do is plough over the same ground in ever deeper furrows' (974); but he finds that circularity 'a strength and not a weakness' for 'if the matter at hand were to be non-circularly described by some point outside it, the matter's intelligibility would hang on something that is not itself intelligible until it was in its turn integrated into a wider unity' (973–5).

If we are to avoid this infinite regress, Weinrib counsels, we must regard the law not so much as 'an instrument in the service of foreign ideals as an end in itself constituting, as it were, its own ideal' (956). Alan Sinfield makes the same point when he says that 'the tendency of a profession is to become self-referential' (*Faultlines*, Berkeley, Los Angeles, 1992, 287), but he makes it as a complaint. Weinrib would reply that in the absence of self-referentiality, one has no grasp of what one is doing or why one is doing it. His example is tort law, which, he says, is best understood as a continuing meditation (by tort law itself) on 'the relationship between tortfeasor and victim' ('Legal Formalism', 969), that is, between someone who wrongfully inflicts an injury and someone who suffers it; and the unfolding of that meditation will necessarily induce considerations of fault, causation, duty, fore-seeability, and proximity. It is always possible, of course, to view a tort case through the lens of some other complex of concerns, let us say the concern to redistribute wealth as evenly as possible independently of any finding of fault or demonstration of loss; but if a case were decided in the name of such a 'foreign ideal', it would be a tort decision in name only, for 'a conception of tort liability in which the plaintiff can recover from the defendant for injury in the absence of wrongdoing, or in which the defendant is liable to the plaintiff for a wrong that does not materialize in injury, would be a "conceptual monstrosity"' (969); that is, it would be employing the language of tort law while bypassing and eviscerating the very rationale (internal and immanent) for there being a tort law in the first place. It would be as if a batter in a baseball game, aware that the opposing pitcher was in jeop-ardy of his job and unhappy at the prospect of depriving someone of his livelihood, chose to strike out rather than advance the run-ner at first base; the criticism properly directed at him would not be that he was playing the game badly, but that he was not play-ing the game at all.

Talk of 'foreign ideals' and 'immanent intelligibility' is of course the language of professionalism, and professionalism is a suspect concept in this era of interdisciplinary hopes. Sinfield complains that the 'profession establishes criteria of what you are supposed to do, and, in that process, questions about the purpose and meaning of the activity drop out of sight' (*Faultlines*, 287). In saying this, Sinfield imagines a process that occurs only once and then immediately congeals into an increasingly unresponsive orthodoxy; but in fact the process of establishing criteria is ongo-ing and is sensitive to both internal and external challenges. New members of the profession, looking with fresh eyes and nascent ambitions at the way things are done, propose changes and thereby initiate debates about 'the purpose and meaning of the activity'; and those same debates can be triggered by those out-side the profession who, for any number of reasons, are in a position to exert pressure on it. (Even so closed a shop as major league baseball, protected by an anti-trust exemption, has been forced by Jesse Jackson and others to examine and alter its hiring patterns in the ranks of managers and front-office personnel.)

To be sure, the obdurate insularity of which Sinfield complains can in fact occur, but when it does it is only a matter of time (perhaps a very long time) before the frustrations and disappointments experienced by both practitioners and laymen issue first in calls, and then in demands, for reform. In most cases, however, reform, in the shape of continual self-modification, is a part of the process. While 'self-referentiality' is, as Sinfield says, a feature of any profession, it is not a static feature; rather, it is an *accomplishment* that is continually renegotiated. A profession confronted with 'new' or unassimilated phenomena will not abandon its immanent intelligibility, but will reassert it either by refusing responsibility for what its categories decline to recognize (here the risk is to be seen as disastrously narrow and therefore without a claim on public support), or by stretching those categories so as to bring within them concerns and materials previously thought to be outside their sphere of competence (as when English studies extended the province of literature to include film, advertising, and even restaurant menus). A profession that takes this second tack will be in danger of losing its shape (by being so inclusive it would no longer be specific), but the danger will be forestalled so long as the internal changes do not add up to a loss of the project's distinctiveness, so long as the key terms in the enterprise are defined by reference to one another and not to the terms of some other enterprise. If this is 'self-referentiality' it is hard to see how a profession, or, indeed, any kind of social activity, could dispense with it without ceasing to be what it is, and this, I take it, is Weinrib's main point.

I want to apply Weinrib's analysis of torts (although with a historicist twist his neo-Kantianism would disdain) to literary interpretation, and I shall begin as he does, by attempting to grasp the sense of purposiveness that animates the practice and generates both the form and content of the gestures appropriate to it. What in the practice of literary interpretation corresponds to the 'fault–cause' nexus in tort law and the imperative of 'winning the game' in baseball? The short (and methodologically unhelpful) answer is that the purpose of literary interpretation is to determine what works of literature mean; and therefore the paradigmatic question in literary criticism is 'What is this poem (or novel or drama) saying?'

The question might sound as if it were launched in the dark and was capable of receiving a wholly surprising answer, but as my discussion of the first line of *Lycidas* has already suggested, the question is asked within the knowledge of what kind of answer might be appropriate. The answer might well be (and indeed, given the reward system of the discipline, had better be) surprising in some respects—it might, for example, aggressively reverse the interpretive direction of previous answers—but in other respects it will have a very recognizable and even obligatory form. It will enhance the work's complexity; it will add to, rather than subtract from, the number of significances the work is thought to bear; it will multiply rather than reduce interpretive problems. In so far as the answer takes this form, it will validate the right of the work to be labelled literary and it will validate the credentials of the commentator, who must show (not tell) that he or she knows what the properties of literariness are, in this case complexity, density, polysemy, multivocality, temporal reversibility, etc.

I am aware that this account of literariness is somewhat dated, and that today the language of 'complexity' and 'density' has been replaced in some quarters by the language of 'fragmentation' and 'rupture'. But the datedness of the account (and of my reading of 'Yet once more') is what makes it useful to the present argument: since as an account it is not currently controversial, I can exhibit it without having to argue for it or defend it. The datedness of the account also has another advantage: it reminds us that literariness is a historical rather than an essential matter.

What is considered 'literary' today was not so considered forty years ago, and literariness either 1995- or 1955-style would not have been describable in the vocabularies of past epochs, vocabularies that often seem to us entirely opaque until we manage, as we usually do, to characterize them as imperfect and primitive versions of what we, in our wisdom, have finally discovered.

Moreover, not only will the category of the literary have different contents at different times (and in different cultures at the same time); there may be times when the category has *no* content, when there is no 'paradigmatic question', and therefore no *literary* interpretation in the exclusive disciplinary sense. If you browse in the eighteenth-century editions of Milton from which I earlier quarried, you will be hard-pressed to say what idea of the literary the editors are following since they are all over the map and seem to include everything, including the proverbial kitchen sink, in their annotations. Much of Warton's commentary concerns itself with the relationship of Milton's poems to other poems it echoes and, presumably, puts itself in competition with: thus we are told that 'west'ring' (line 31) is 'A word that occurs in Chaucer' and that when Milton describes the dancing of 'Rough Satyrs', the 'like effects' are 'ascribed to Silenus' by Virgil in his sixth eclogue and is picked up too by the author of a contemporary elegy on the death of Philip Sidney, who was, not incidentally, a veritable type of the poet in the late sixteenth and early seventeenth centuries. Other lines in the poem occasion lengthy accounts of the geography of the regions to which Milton refers. Still others argue fine points of grammar and debate with previous commentators the proper positioning of commas. Syntactic analysis, biographical speculation, influence study, political allegory, the taxonomy of streams and rivers, arcane points of mythology—all are cheerfully offered up with no particular emphasis or sense of ordering.

One might say that this is, after all, a variorum edition, and that is what the editors of such editions do; but the makers of the twentieth-century variorum (still in progress) have a more consecutive sense of their task; their notes, while fully responsive to the antiquarian spirit of the genre, also track interpretive problems as they have been established in the review of criticism that prefaces the annotations proper. In contrast, even when the eighteenth-century editors produce essays rather than footnotes, their writing retains the emphasis on discrete observations made in the absence of any apparent pressure to produce a *reading*. It is the assumed pre-eminence of readings, in the sense of extended and coherent interpretations, that accounts for the features of twentieth-century 'literariness' as I earlier indexed them: complexity, density, multivocality, etc. The poetic we have inherited from Coleridge and Poe (the poetic of Romanticism) imagines literary productions as objects of a very particular kind—self-contained, densely layered, and saturated with a kind of meaning that can only be teased out by interpreters with special skills.

In contrast, the eighteenth-century editors and commentators show almost no interest in meaning except when a particular passage displays an obscurity that can presumably be removed by the application of a piece of biographical knowledge or a learned exercise in lexicography. Meaning, that (appropriately) elusive object of twentieth-century exegesis, is simply assumed by annotators, who see their task as pointing out the beauties or infelicities of a poetic performance that is being judged against the background of past performances of a similar kind. In so far as there is an aesthetic dimension to the evaluation, it takes the form of invoking a fixed set of categories and asking how the present writer measures up to a norm that has been established by his predecessors. Are the characters finely drawn? Is there a pleasing variety in the number and kinds of persons a reader encounters? Does the fable (roughly, plot) display the appropriate mixture of probability and marvellous occurrence as recommended by Aristotle? Do the similes rise to a great idea and thus display the sublimity 'which is suitable to the Nature of An Heroick Poem' (Joseph Addison, in J. Shawcross, ed., *Milton: The Critical Heritage up to 1731*, London, 1970, 172)?

[27]

These and other questions are asked in a way suggesting it is obligatory to pose them; and they are answered not by the extended analyses familiar to us as the students (and indeed products) of the New Criticism, but with general words of approbation and (more occasionally) of disapprobation. Addison, who generally comes to praise not to bury his subject, typically refrains from giving reasons for his judgements, saying again and again that the excellence he has just affirmed is too perspicuous to require comment. 'I need not Point out the Beauty of that Circumstance' (*Critical Heritage*, 179). Indeed to the late twentieth-century ear or eye, Addison is engaged not in criticism, but in cheer-leading of a kind we now associate with the journalistic reviewers of the popular press.

In writing this last sentence I have fallen in (almost involuntarily) with the prejudices built into the professional practice of which I am a member. It is hard when reading the critical texts of another age to see anything but what is so obviously (from your present vantage-point) missing. Commenting on Servius' commentary on Virgil's eclogues (no doubt known to Milton and, we can assume, an influence on him as he wrote *Lycidas*), R. R. Bolgar complains that 'one cannot fail to be struck by the almost complete absence from the notes of any discussion on the wider problems of aesthetics and literary form' (*The Classical Heritage and Its Beneficiaries*, Cambridge, 1954; repr. New York, 1964, 41). What I have been suggesting is that 'the wider problems of aesthetics and literary form' may not have been problems for Servius or, later, for Addison and Warton. One suspects too that 'problems' is a particularly powerful word for Bolgar (as it would be for me) because it is so central to the very definition of what literature, as distinct from other activities, is *for* in the mind of a modern critic. The purpose of literature, we have come to believe, is to problematize, to disturb the settled surface of commonly received truths. John Beverley is only one of the more recent theorists to proclaim that we 'tend to think of literature as a sanctioned space for the expression of social dissidence' (*Against*

[28]

Literature, Minneapolis, 1993, 25). Given this view of literature's purpose (which I do not here endorse, but merely report), interpretive crises are noted not so that they can be solved, but so they can be multiplied, and a critic understands that it is his job to leave more problems (and more dissidence) than he found.

No wonder then that we find it so difficult to come to terms with a criticism that seems to operate on the model of housecleaning, polishing a bit of the furniture here, removing unwanted cobwebs and constellations of dust there. Where, we ask, is the strenuous act of imagination that strives to match the act performed by the poet? Where is the strong sense of methodology and of interpretive paths that are taken not randomly but under the pressure of a self-consciously wielded 'theory' of art? Where, in short, is the *argument*, that linear exercise in demonstrative reasoning that signals to critics and readers alike, 'This is literary interpretation'. What the eighteenth-century commentaries seem to say is, 'Anything is literary interpretation'—biography, parsing of grammar, etymology, philology, political commentary, geography, etc., and if this is so, then it is not too much to say that for them *nothing* is literary interpretation, for there is no observation about a text of Milton's or Virgil's in response to which a member of the culture would immediately object, 'That's not the kind of thing we do around here'.

Today, of course, there is no end of argument about the precise parameters of 'what we do around here'; but those who engage in the argument push against a sense of boundaries strongly (some would say too strongly) in place. The fact that there are disputes about literary studies is less significant than the fact that the disputes are about something assumed to possess its own rationale and therefore to have achieved 'immanent intelligibility'. It is an achievement, however, that brings with it a considerable cost; for if, from the vantage-point of a shared expertise, we can now intelligibly say 'That's not the kind of thing we do around here', we are without defence when someone turns around and says to us, 'Your specialized skills have no claim on our attention, for that's not the kind of thing *we* do around *here'*. As late twentieth-century literary actors we may feel qualified to perform when there is a call for informed opinions about *Paradise Lost* or *King Lear*, but our ability to so perform does not qualify us to intervene in a political or economic crisis.

No armed guard, however, would have stopped Milton, Spenser, Sidney, or Raleigh at the palace gate or the door of the parliament because they had only written poems, and indeed the *literary* achievements of these authors would have provided them with a ticket of entry to the 'wider' realms of social and political life, especially in the context of a patronage system presided over by a court that was as much a cultural and theological institution as it was the seat of government. We must remember that Queen Elizabeth and James I had literary lives; that is, they were, or claimed to be, *producers* of literature and they were certainly central figures in the productions of the poets and dramatists who sought to win their favour. If someone should today aim for a position in government or commerce or aspire to become an ambassador to a foreign court, he or she (it would have earlier been only 'he') would not think to further that ambition by writing a poem or a sequence of sonnets, but that is exactly what Sidney, Ben Jonson, and Donne did. In their world a poem celebrating the king's birthday or a lord's ascendancy to high office—poems we now condescendingly label 'occasional'—is more than an early version of a Hallmark greeting card; it is an affirmation of the 'rightness' of things as embodied in a reciprocal set of mutual recognitions. The poet recognizes (and re-announces) the legitimacy of the king and his counsellors; they recognize (and welcome) an affirmation whose compliment they return by accepting it; everyone is playing his role in an ongoing enterprise that does not pose insiders against outsiders, but rather includes insiders differently positioned and differently employed.

Once this nicely reciprocal relationship between literary activity and a court eager to see its legitimacy and accomplishments reflected back to it is no longer in place, it becomes a question as to what poets are supposed to do and for whom they are to do it. When the answer arrives in the form of the Romantic emphasis on inspiration and the attendant de-emphasis of social and political factors, the result is a splendid isolation that finds a place for poetry, but one that is literally out of this world. The artist now communicates not with princes and with lords but with other artists in a realm even more élite than the Elizabethan court. The circuit of communication now goes not from poet to patron (and back again) but from poet to peer and to a small group of readers whose sensibility is answerable to that visionary company. The difference between this conception of 'literariness' and the one it replaces can be seen by recalling Milton's famous invocation of 'fit audience though few', which bears a superficial resemblance to the exclusiveness of Romantic aestheticism. But the fitness of Milton's wished-for audience is not aesthetic but moral and political, and it is a fitness matching that of the poet who, Milton says in the *Apology*, can hope to 'write well' only if he himself is a 'true Poem, that is a composition and patterne of the best and honourablest things; not presuming to sing high praises of heroick men, or famous cities, unlesse he have in himself the experience and the practice of all that is praiseworthy' (*The Complete Prose Works of John Milton*, ed. Don Wolfe *et al.*, New Haven, 1953, i. 890).

This means exactly what it says: poetic value is a function of personal and civic virtue; the man who fashions an artful line but does so with a malign intention or with an insufficient sense of the public weal will have produced unworthy poetry. Whereas in modern aesthetics form is prior to content and technique is the focus of evaluation, in Milton's view technique detached from 'pure and sublime thoughts' is empty and meretricious; only an interior beauty—a beauty of the spirit—will issue in truly beautiful language. One can gauge the distance between this and the more contemporary view by listening to Camille Paglia when she declares that even if he had gunned down ten grandmothers, Picasso would have been a great artist. Milton would have found such a statement inconceivable, as would have Ben Jonson, Augustine, Minturno, Cicero, and countless others who voiced what was for a long time the commonplace conviction that art is measured by the extent which it proceeds from and inculcates moral behaviour.

In our time the relationship between art and the production of civic virtue is thin to the point of vanishing. At most one can claim, with Shelley, that poets are the unacknowledged legislators of the world; the ambition is grand, but it is much more abstract and less capable of verification than the ambition felt and sometimes realized by poets whose influence on the acknowledged legislators was defining of their project. Deprived of a secure if unofficial place in the corridors of government and commerce, literary activity is increasingly pursued in the academy where proficiency is measured by academic standards and rewarded by the gatekeepers of an academic guild. The name for this is professionalization, a form of organization in which membership is acquired by a course of special training whose end is the production of persons who recognize one another not because they regularly meet at the same ceremonial occasions (unless one equates an MLA meeting with the Elizabethan court), but because they perform the same 'moves' in the same 'game'. That is, they participate in the same 'immanent intelligibility' whose content is the same set of 'internal'—not foreign—purposes.

It would not be too much to say that these purposes are exactly the opposite of those informing the intelligibility of literary activity before the Enlightenment. The 'foreign ideals' against which the literary—from both the production and consumption ends—now defines itself are the very ideals that would have been named as internal and constitutive by someone like Milton: contribution to civic harmony and public aspiration, guidance to princes and generals, education of the children of the ruling class, celebration of royal birthdays, inculcation of religious sentiments. All of these are now understood (except by new historicists and cultural materialists) as appropriate to the purposes animating *other* enterprises: politics, warfare, educational planning, theology.

Here I can imagine someone saying 'those were the days' and urging us to work for the reintegration of the literary with the political and the social. To that urging I would respond, first, that it's not that easy, and, second, that even if a reintegration should somehow be effected, it would not compromise or blur the distinctiveness of tasks as I have been arguing for it. My introduction of a historical dimension at this point should not be taken to suggest that if we could only recover the conditions obtaining in the Renaissance, literary activity and political activity could again be one and the same. They were not one and the same then. To be sure, in the sixteenth and seventeenth centuries literary actors could *also* be political actors, and could, as part of their political activity, make use of their literary credentials; but even when they did so, they had a strong sense of distinctive abilities whose exercise could at times be put into a double harness. For Milton and the others, even in their state of cultural integration, thinking to compose a poem was an act conditioned by the history and presupposed imperatives of poetic practice as embodied in the texts of accepted exemplars (Virgil, Homer, etc.). What distinguishes them from us is that they could then contemplate incorporating that literary intention into a political one by, say, writing a poem intended to influence military or diplomatic policy. They would then be putting to political effect a competence that was not, in and of itself, political at all. In short, they could reasonably intervene in political matters by exercising literary skills. In so far as there survives any sense of the literary as an interventionary project, it takes the form of a claim that it is the purpose of the literary to provide a space of critique—a vantage-point of clear-eyed, astringent interrogation—from which the apparent coherence of familiar discourses can be problematized and challenged. But in this view of literary effectivity the work is understood to be done at the level of conceptual analysis and does not involve the urging of any particular agenda, except the agenda of continual sceptical scrutiny.

That is why the pre-eminent question of literary interpretation—what does this poem (or novel or play) *mean?*—is properly answered not by a proposition ('This poem means that war is hell' or 'This poem means that infant mortality is a national disgrace'), but by a *refusal directly to answer it*. Something must always be left over, unaccounted for, open to still another turn of the interpretive screw; were this not so, the work could be said to have engaged in totalizing—in telling (or claiming to tell) the truth about the world once and for all—and thereby forfeited its right to be called 'literary'. To be sure, literary works are full of propositions of the kind one finds in philosophy or history ('This is so' or 'This is what happened'), but in a literary performance, either at the production end or at the reception end, propositions and accounts of facts do not come into primary focus; rather they provide the material, or 'stuff', on which the literary impulse— the impulse to probe ever deeper the incorrigible duplicity of assertion even as it presents itself as univocal and single—can be exercised. (I hasten to say again that I am not here giving my own answer to the question 'What is literature?', but reporting on the answer most practitioners would today give if they were asked.)

In so distinguishing the literary or literariness from the workings of philosophy and history respectively I may have reminded you of an earlier effort along the same lines. In his *Defense of Poesy*, Philip Sidney identifies philosophy with the giving of general precepts and opposes it to history, which offers us an undifferentiated mass of particular examples. It is the excellence of the poet, says Sidney, to do *both* 'for whatsoever the philosopher says should be done, he gives a perfect picture of it by someone by whom he presupposes it was done, so as he couples the general notion with the particular example' (*Sir Philip Sidney's* Defense of Poesy, ed. Lewis Soens, Lincoln, Nebr., 1970, 17). Like his modern counterpart, then, Sidney puts poetry in a special category, but there is a crucial difference. Whereas twentieth-century critics distinguish poetry from history and philosophy in order to sequester artistic production and reception from the contingencies of politics, Sidney locates poetry's distinctiveness in its superior ability to prosecute a moral/political task. In his account philosophy, history, and poetry are all in the same line of public work—telling and promulgating the truth; it is just that poetry does it better, 'not only . . . furnishing the mind with knowledge, but . . . setting it forward to that which deserves to be called and accounted good', for 'it is not knowing, but doing must be the fruit' (23).

By linking poetry so strongly to action, Sidney implicitly authorizes poets (and literary people in general) to intervene in the realm of public affairs, where they might perform as advisers to princes, as ambassadors, as churchmen, as legislators, as diplomats, as the leaders of commercial and military expeditions, in short, in all the ways taken up by Sidney, Spenser, Raleigh, Donne, Marvell, and Milton. One should note that this expansive understanding of the arenas into which poets can intrude themselves has as its corollary a correspondingly expansive understanding of the dangers awaiting them in those arenas. Service to a king or a prelate, even if it is largely verbal, carries with it risks (of dismissal, banishment, incarceration, death) from which the poet as Sidney conceives him cannot be insulated. In 1992 by contrast, insulation is assured (who *cares* what poets do?) but at the price of the wide entry and influence to which Sidney and his friends could reasonably aspire.

This shift from an aesthetic that puts poetry in the world to one that quarantines it is accompanied by (and reflected in) a shift in attitudes toward censorship. Even so staunch a defender of free expression as Milton protested only against 'prior restraint', the suppressing of speech or writing before it appears on the world's stage; once something has been published, however, 'it is of greatest concernment in the church and commonwealth, to have a vigilant eye how books demean themselves as well as men; and therefore to confine, imprison, and do sharpest justice on them as malefactors' (*Areopagitica*). What will seem strange to the modern reader of this passage is the absence of the distinction between action, the proper object of judicial attention, and expression which, because it is merely verbal and without real-world consequences, should be exempt from regulation. It is this distinction that Milton specifically rejects, insisting on the 'potency' of words no less than of deeds and therefore holding them to a standard of accountability that not only allows but demands state scrutiny. To do otherwise, he would have said, would be to imply that verbal actions do not matter or that they matter only in a realm wholly distanced from political life, a realm called, perhaps, 'the life of the mind' or 'the world of the imagination'.

This of course is exactly what is not merely implied but stated in many twentieth-century accounts of the matter: verbal productions except when they cross a line and become incitements to action—and when they cross that line they cease to be truly expressive or truly literary—are to be regarded as the effusions of essentially free minds; and therefore any attempt to police them is an infringement upon that freedom. The development of this argument, which is at the heart of liberalism's disinclination either to authorize or to condemn anyone's opinions, has provided the artist with his strongest bulwark against state regulation (although, as many would complain, it is a bulwark continually being breached by overreaching statists), but at the same time the argument deprives the artist of any rationale for intervening in precincts that have been assigned to other agents whose franchise is held no less exclusively than his.

It is by now a familiar paradox: artistic freedom is purchased at the expense of artistic efficacy. As Norman Mailer has put it,

Every gain of freedom carries its price. There's a wonderful moment when you go from oppression to freedom, there in the middle, when one's still oppressed but one's achieved the first freedoms. There's an extraordinary period that goes from there until the freedoms begin to outweigh the oppression. By the time you get over to complete free-

dom, you begin to look back almost nostalgically on the days of oppression, because in those days you were ready to become a martyr, you
had a sense of importance, you could take yourself seriously, you were
fighting the good fight. (Quoted in Edward de Grazia, *Girls Lean Back
Everywhere: The Law of Obscenity and the Assault on Genius*, New York,
1992, 495.)

Recently, Mailer's words have been echoed (and confirmed) by
Russian poet Aleksandr Kushner. In the good old days, Kushner
explains, the writer was 'like an uncrowned prince'. Now, he
laments, 'this is gone':

Why? In those days, literature was the one real door open to people of
a certain kind. Now there are lots of doors to walk through. You can go
into business, play on the Israeli soccer team, play for a New York
hockey team, make your fortune in Greece, or even go into politics if
you choose. At the same time, literature in the eyes of many has lost its
exceptional importance. Literature will always have a place, as it does
in America. Marginal, but important. Small but beautiful. Of course, if
a monster, a fascist, like Vladimir Zhironovsky is ever elected President
of Russia, literature might have to assume its old role. But for now, no.
(*New Yorker*, 18 July 1994, 52)

Notice that in Kushner's mind the resumption by literature of its
'old role' will have to wait upon events external to the literary
culture. If the battle for artistic freedom has been won, but is now
seen to bring with it losses that had not been contemplated, you
cannot, by yourself or in the company of your fellows, turn back
the clock and reinstitute the condition (of there being a good
fight to fight) that once gave your project its excitement and con-
sequentiality. Turning the clock back would not be the preferred
self-description of those who call today for a more interventionary literary scholarship; but it is no accident that such calls
often issue from scholars who work in the sixteenth and seventeenth centuries and who have argued, persuasively in my view,
for an Elizabethan–Jacobean culture in which the boundaries
between the literary and non-literary are permeable. What
is curious is that the insights of these scholars into the material

conditions which made intervention possible and even inescapable in the period they study have not been matched by a recognition that these conditions no longer exist and a realization that their return cannot be willed either by an individual or by the collective of a gathered practice. If no one critic can, by himself, declare a change in the basic gestures by which he signals and validates his entry into an ongoing practice, no one practice can, by itself, rearrange the map of responsibilities, efficacies, relevancies, and possible consequences that marks out the spheres assigned (by no one and everyone) to all the games currently in play. Any announcement by one of these practices that it will now enlarge the territory within which its agents are understood to operate will be met with resistance and incredulity.

Imagine, if you will, a meeting of all the literary and cultural critics in the world at a single conference, and imagine an overwhelming vote to the effect that from now on we shall address our analyses not to the small number of our professional peers but to the public at large and that we expect an alerted public to pay us the kind of attention it mistakenly reserves for politicians, political pundits, and basketball players. Such a proclamation would have its brief moment of impact as newspapers reported on one more instance of academic hubris and absurdity; but when the laughter had died down, little, if anything, will have changed. This is not to say that the division of labour and its attendant parcelling out of responsibilities and rewards cannot be changed, only that the change will be structural, effected not by an isolated act of will, whether performed by an individual or by the collective of a particular practice, but by shifts in the cultural consciousness that are glacially slow and overdetermined. This point is not understood by those like Bruce Robbins who believe that because literary criticism has shifted (at least in some avant-garde quarters) from an aesthetic to a socio-political justification of its project, it is now 'able to claim a more public role' (*Secular Vocations*, London, 1993, 97). This internal change (were it to be effected on a large scale, a matter still in doubt) will certainly alter both the rhetoric and the practice of criticism, but it will not alter the world, unless the world has been altered already. Criticism can 'claim' anything it likes; it can claim to be a cure for the common cold; but making good on its claims will depend on forces it cannot even muster, never mind control.

Disciplinary Tasks and Political Intentions

IN our previous meetings I set out to consider the claims and hopes of those who believe that literary criticism can be made to engage directly and effectively with the project of restructuring the whole of modern society. I began by offering as an example of mainstream literary analysis an elaborate (but by no means exhaustive) reading of the first three words of Milton's *Lycidas*, 'Yet once more'. After completing as much of the analysis as either you or I could bear I stepped back to ask what it is that I had done, how I had been able to do it, and how it is that you were able to understand it, whether or not you agreed with the details of my performance. I found the answer not in the text itself, but in the conventional and obligatory routines that are the content of literary work for those who have been initiated into its practice. Those routines, I contended, identify literary work as a distinctive enterprise, one that has title to a certain set of concerns as they are brought to light and into focus by a certain set of questions, the questions I employed unreflectively in my reading of 'Yet once more'.

My point was that unless an enterprise is undergirded by a sense of the questions appropriate to it, it will have no proper shape. In order to sharpen the point, I made a brief excursion into the area of tort law or the law of negligence. Taking my cue from the writing of Ernest Weinrib, I argued that the very concept of negligence required one to be concerned with a limited set of issues: issues of cause (is the defendant responsible for the injury suffered by the plaintiff?), issues of fault (is the causal link between the defendant's action and the plaintiff's injury one that was in his control? could he have exercised due care in order to avoid it?), issues of proximity (was the effect of the defendant's action one he could have anticipated or was it so etiolated and mediated that he could not have reasonably been expected to have it in mind at the moment of acting?). If these and related issues are set aside, as some have wanted to do, and replaced by a universal insurance scheme, by a regime of either strict liability or no-fault liability, the result would not be the *reform* of negligence law but the *abandonment* of negligence law for something else, and this would hold true even if that something else continued to be called negligence law. Literary criticism, I asserted, is likewise characterized by a limited set of concerns and if those concerns are replaced by some others and the questions internal to literary study—questions like 'What does this poem mean?'—are let go in favour of other, supposedly larger, questions, one would still be doing something, but it would not be literary criticism.

I hastened to add that the distinctive shape of literary work, as I described it, was not stable over time, and that, indeed, in earlier periods literary work had no distinctive shape to speak of and was continuous, as some now want it to be again, with social, economic, and political work. In the sixteenth and seventeenth centuries, for example, the boundaries between the literary and the 'extra-literary' were not at all firm and it was quite possible for poets and literary pamphleteers to enter other arenas and to present as their qualifications for entrance their literary skills and accomplishments. The down side of this relatively easy commerce was an inability to say of literary work that it was a particular thing and not everything. There was no strong sense of a discipline or a profession with its well-developed credentialling procedures and ways of distinguishing sharply between insiders and outsiders. The emergence of the *profession* of literary studies is thus a recent accomplishment of roughly the last 100 years, but the accomplishment has not been without its costs and the chief cost has been the increasing difficulty of connecting up specific-ally literary work with the larger arenas in which it was once able to intervene. One may reasonably lament this loss, but one can-not reasonably, I argue, will it away or undo it by changing the object of one's literary attention from poems to television shows or by changing the name of the literary enterprise to, say, cultural studies. It follows, given this analysis of our present situation, that the desire of new historicists and cultural critics to turn the clock back will continue to be frustrated.

That, at any rate, is my thesis, and in today's lecture I will pros-ecute it by turning directly to the new historicism and its discon-tents. Before doing so, however, I want to make one final point born out of a fear that my strictures against the possibility of a truly political criticism might give comfort to some people with whom I disagree even more than I disagree with the Alan Sinfields of this world. In a review of Sinfield's *Faultlines* (*Sunday Telegraph*, 25 October 1992; Oxford University Press, Oxford, and Berkeley, Los Angeles, 1992), Blair Worden complains that the book shouldn't have been published because it detracts from the love and appreciation of literature and contributes only to the increasing marginalization of literary studies. The trouble, he says, is that literary criticism is not really an academic discipline; it is, rather, an 'intuitive and imaginative gift' which does not flour-ish when harnessed to the 'artificial and insulated language' of aca-demic pretensions. My argument is exactly the reverse: literary criticism is *only*, today, an academic discipline and the specialized language of which Worden complains is the mark of its distinc-tiveness and its franchise. From my perspective Sinfield and Worden are in the same line of work; both want to get beyond the current professionalization of literary studies to something else, to radical political work in Sinfield's case and to the celebration of the texts that embody and preserve our highest values in Worden's case. They are alike political, and even politically correct, albeit in different directions. I am *professionally* correct, not out of a sense of moral obligation or choice of values—there is no moral dimension to my position at all (I am not urging a practice, but reporting on the imperatives built into a practice), and certainly no choice—but out of a sense that the structure of a fully articulated profession, be it negligence law or literary criticism, is such that those who enter its precincts will find that the basic decisions, about where to look, what to do, and how to do it, have already been made.

As many of you will know, I have made arguments like this before and they have drawn the wrath of those who are committed to the project of transforming literary studies into a politically emancipatory activity. Sinfield, for example, attributes to me the view that 'academics are limited to the "particular game" and the "constitutive rules" established in the profession', and replies indignantly (one can almost hear him stamping his feet), 'this is not true: we can bend, stretch, violate, and extend the rules in all kinds of ways' (*Faultlines*, 289). Well, yes and no. One can, in fact, bend, stretch, violate, and extend the rules in all kinds of ways, but not in any old way, for what constitutes a stretch or even a violation will be a function of the rules, or, as I would prefer to say, senses of appropriateness currently in place. If the stretch or violation 'takes', there will be a new understanding of the profession's decorums, but those decorums will still be specific to the profession's practice, which will be internally altered, but not necessarily altered in its relationship to other practices, like the practice of politics, from which it will continue to be distinguished. I may propose a reading of a poem that modifies previous readings, or I may propose a reading of a poem that will strike others as perfectly outlandish, or I may even propose that we no longer read poems but instead read the cultural conditions that produce their intelligibility, but these stretchings, bendings, and violations will not in themselves cause my readings to resonate in quarters beyond the confines of the academy. Changing the mode of literary analysis or changing the object of literary analysis or changing the name of literary analysis will not change the material effectiveness of literary analysis and make it into an instrument of political action. That kind of change, if it is ever to occur, will require wholesale *structural* changes of which literary analysts might take advantage, but which they could never initiate.

Of course there are many today who regard their efforts as contributing to just such a wholesale, transformative, change. In the United States they are often called new historicists, although the name is less important than the claim often associated with it (and with cultural studies in general) to be altering the world by doing a new kind of academic literary work. There are as many definitions of new historicism as there are practitioners (many of whom now disavow the label in the manner of the McCarthy hearings: 'I am not now, nor have ever been . . .'), and rather than begin with my own, let me rehearse some of the arguments of an early and influential exemplar. In his justly admired *The Country and the City* (New York, 1973) Raymond Williams (more a cultural materialist than a new historicist, strictly speaking) offers an account of the pastoral quite deliberately at odds with the one I have employed (and assumed) in the preceding pages. Noting the persistence into the seventeenth century of the image of 'a simple community living on narrow margins and experiencing the delights of summer and fertility' (15), Williams reads the poetry that delivers that image as part of an effort to divert its readers from paying attention to 'what the country was really like' (18), a landscape of misery, pain, and exploitation. Moreover, he adds, twentieth-century scholars who prate on about the 'pastoral tradition' are complicit in this strategy of avoidance, perpetuating in their commentaries the scandalous substitution for the 'visible reality' (22) of agrarian conditions the myth of an 'enamelled world' (18). Rather than raising questions about the adequacy of the poetic portrayal to the material facts of rural existence, they content themselves with the 'confident glossing and glozing of the reference back' (18) to Horace, Virgil, Hesiod, and, of course Theocritus. In the process they fail to remember or emphasize 'that Sidney's *Arcadia*, which gives a continuing title to English neo-pastoral, was written in a park which had been made by enclosing a whole village and evicting the tenants' (22).

It is important to realize that Williams is not merely urging scholars to approach literary materials from a new angle; he is asking them to confront the implications of their practice in ways that do not allow them to think of it as 'merely literary': 'There is only one real question. Where do we stand, with whom do we identify . . . ? Is it with the serfs, the bordars and cotters, the villeins; or with the abstracted order to which, through successive generations, many hundreds of thousands of men were never more than instrumental?' (38). Here the choice of what kind of criticism to write is indistinguishable from the choice of what kind of political stance we shall strike and with what consequences. Shall we identify with the regime of 'agrarian capitalism' (22) that feeds on an underclass that is then written out of ideological representations in which (as in Jonson's *To Penshurst*) fish and game and young girls offer themselves eagerly for consumption? Or shall we rather recover the elided perspective of the victim and refuse the lures of an easy idealization? This moral challenge demands that we acknowledge the extent to which *scholarly* labours, like any other, are implicated in a structure of interests and manipulations. In so far as the effects of the ideology Williams uncovers continue into this very day (as he believes they do), every failure to combat it, even in the supposedly sequestered groves of the academy (another, indeed the same, form of pastoral self-deception), is a perpetuation of it and of its evils. Critics who complacently re-rehearse the 'story of pastoral' from Theocritus to the present, as if it were a story only of increasingly mannered imitations and small modifications within a field rigorously and safely aesthetic, become accomplices of the politics served by that story; while those who resist the lure of its surfaces and lay bare the motives of its producers and consumers pursue quite another politics, one that leads from the illusions projected by a sanitized and enamelled myth to the truth of things as they really are.

This is heady stuff, not least because of the new weight (and chance for glory) it places upon acts of literary analysis. No longer, if we accept the strongest versions of the new historicism, are the effects of such acts confined to the narrow precincts (classrooms, learned journals, scholarly monographs) in which they typically occur; rather, they reach out to impact the larger culture that allows them a place but can itself be altered by what it allows. Even if it is the expectation of the culture (as represented by state legislators, trustees, boards of regents, secretaries of education, etc.) that literary critics, along with other humanist scholars, will transmit and refurbish its favourite presuppositions, that expectation can be disappointed by those who decide to 'read against the grain' with a view toward troubling and eventually dislodging the forms of thought that support the prevailing system of received opinion. It is by such strategies of subversive reading, Louis Montrose explains, that we can make the 'politics of the academy extend beyond that we casually refer to as "academic politics"', for 'by choosing to foreground in my readings of Shakespeare or Spenser such issues as the politics of gender, the contestation of cultural constraints, the social instrumentality of writing and playing, I am not only engaged in our necessary and continuous re-invention of Elizabethan culture, but I am also endeavoring to make that engagement participate in the re-formation of our own' ('Professing the Renaissance', in H. Aram Veeser, ed., *The New Historicism*, New York, 1989, 30).

This is a rich and interesting statement and one that invites and rewards interrogation. First of all, what exactly does Montrose mean by 'choose'? On its face he seems to be saying something like this: 'I have surveyed the various approaches to Shakespeare and Spenser now in play and have decided to employ in my own work those (like gender studies) that will be the most subversive of the political powers now oppressing us.' But when I read Montrose I find his analyses informed by a conviction that the accounts he offers of Shakespeare and Spenser are true. He may believe that by producing these *true* accounts he will be participating in the reformation of contemporary society, but his belief in their possible political efficacy is independent of his conviction that they are true. Were he to be persuaded that there was no particular political benefit to be had from putting forward these views of Shakespeare and Spenser, they would still be his views, and they would remain so until they were changed by the usual kinds of argument one associates with literary studies. It is surely the case that his views of Shakespeare and Spenser *could* change, but one thing that won't change them (if they are really his views and not merely politically convenient sentiments) is the realization that they aren't doing the kind of political work he hoped they would do. (What might change, if he experienced that realization, is his determination to remain a professional reader of texts; he might get into another line of work.)

All of which is to say that one doesn't 'choose' one's readings; one is *persuaded* to them, and one is persuaded to them not by calculating their political effects, but by coming up with answers to questions that are constitutive of the present practice of producing readings. No doubt Montrose believed something about Spenser and Shakespeare before he believed that they could best be read in the light of gender politics or cultural conflict; and no doubt, too, whatever it is he believed in this previous state emerged in the course of his moving within the traditions of inquiry into which he had been initiated by his instructors and by the course of reading he pursued in directions that were marked as relevant within the professional context of his labours; and no doubt (finally) it was by virtue of those same markers of relevance that he was provoked to look in other places for new ways of prosecuting his task—the task, as he acknowledges, of producing readings—and to new ways of presenting and justifying the results.

My point, already made, is that all this transpired *within* and not in opposition to the normal routines of the discipline's business, routines that are at once open, in that they accommodate themselves to novelty, and closed, in that the aftermath of accommodation is a reconfiguration and not an elimination of a disciplinary boundary. Not only does Montrose not *choose* to read Shakespeare and Spenser in the manner he now does, but those readings are not oppositional in any strong sense because the very conceiving of them depended on the prior availability and *authority* of conventional forms of thought, forms of thought that are constitutive of the alternative paths a would-be reader of Shakespeare and Spenser might consider taking or (it amounts to the same thing) might consider refusing.

The other side of this is the obligation of someone who pursues a path or refuses it in favour of another to justify the result (if asked) by invoking those same constitutive forms of thought as the basis of giving and weighing evidence. Why, someone might ask Montrose, do you read Shakespeare and Spenser in gender terms, and if the answer were 'because I know that such readings will drive William Bennett and Lynne Cheney crazy' he would be understood to be putting the cart before the horse. Driving Lynne Cheney and William Bennett crazy might be the happily unintended consequence of a reading, but it cannot be directly productive of a reading because you could not begin with the intention of driving Lynne Cheney and William Bennett crazy and produce *any* reading of Shakespeare and Spenser without supplementing that intention with the regular machinery of literary criticism, the machinery whose operations lead to conclusions as to what a literary work is about. A serious (as opposed to a flippant) answer to the question 'Why do you read Shakespeare and Spenser in gender terms?' would involve, for example, elaborating a correlation between scenes in Shakespeare and Spenser and contemporary treatises on the family, or documenting the pervasive and multiform effects in a society of having a female monarch presiding over a male-dominated court, or rehearsing (yet once more) the many strains of Petrarchianism and anti-Petrarchianism that furnished so much of the social and sexual vocabulary of the day. All of these, and many other, possible responses would identify Montrose as a literary person speaking to other literary persons in terms that would be immediately comprehensible to the relevant parties but not to those for whom the entire culture of literary studies was a mystery at best and a scam at worst.

My thesis is a simple one: in order to produce something that would count as a reading, Montrose, like everyone else, has to pose questions that are recognizably literary and give answers in terms that would make sense to literary actors, even if those answers were contested by some of his peers. Therefore, his interpretive act will not be a political one except in the narrow sense he rejects: i.e. it participates in academic politics, in the (internal) politics of Shakespeare and Spenser studies. One must distinguish between the general (and trivial) sense in which everything is political—the sense in which every action is ultimately rooted in a contestable point of origin—and the more usual sense of 'political' when the word is used to refer to actions performed with the intention of winning elections or influencing legislators. Giving an account of what you believe to be true of a literary work, even if it is controversial, is not political in this second sense. Of course giving an account of a literary work may have a political effect (in the unlikely event, for example, that Bill Clinton picks it up and factors it into his thinking), but an effect like that can hardly be what you have in mind when you set about crafting your account. (It is not only that you can't count on it, but that there are other more direct routes to take if you want to influence Bill Clinton.) The point is tautological, but it is a tautology with a bite: you cannot engage in a disciplinary performance without thinking of yourself as performing in *that* way and not in some other.

But suppose that Montrose or someone else managed to finesse that psychological state and put forward a reading solely because it furthered his political (as opposed to disciplinary) purposes. Suppose, in short, that someone did, in fact, *choose* a reading in the sense I have challenged and then dressed it up (as he would have to do for it to be received as a reading) in disciplinary clothing; what would then follow? Very little, I think. The critic who engaged in that charade—pretending to be in the literary criticism business while really being in the business of partisan politics—might have to bear the burden of insincerity (although he could no doubt salve his conscience by telling himself that he was acting out of 'higher motives'), but his performance would fail of its intended effect (although as I have already noted it might have that effect accidentally), assuming that the intended effect was something more than changing someone's mind about what is going on in Shakespeare and Spenser. The reason it would fail is that, as things stand now in our society, interpretations of literary works, no matter what their emphasis and independently of the motives of those who produce them, do not connect up strongly with the issues being debated in the larger political arena. Given the lines of communication and power now in place there is just too much distance between the mode of presentation and argument specific to literary criticism and the mode of presentation and argument in public forums (legislative, journalistic, juridical) to allow a direct (or even strongly indirect) line of influence between them, even when, at some level, the concerns are pretty much the same.

An interpretation of *Othello* that marks out the dynamics of race-consciousness in a manner that might gain it publication in *Representations* is not in itself going to constitute an effective intervention in our anguished national conversation about race; and an analysis of gender reversals in *Macbeth* or *Coriolanus* will not move members of the public, wherever they might be situated, to rethink the case for or against abortion. What this means is that both the fear provoked by the new historicism, that it will lead to the substitution of partisan political agendas for the decorums and standards thought proper to the academy, and the hope attached to the new historicism, that it will lead to the substitution of partisan political agendas for the decorums and standards thought proper to the academy, are jointly unrealizable; the fear because performances in the academy must take a certain obligatory form; the hope because the form academic performances take, whether it is achieved 'sincerely' or as a matter of strategy, will not allow those performances to be effective outside the very special precincts of the academic world.

Let me say at once that this is a fact not about academic labours in general, but about the labours of literary interpreters. It is not simply by virtue of its location in the university that literary criticism is denied influence in the society; it is because there are, at present, no well-established routes by which literary criticism is first brought to the attention of those who inhabit the centres of power and then presented to them in a way that ties it to their concerns. This is not the case, however, for other kinds of academics who, for a variety of reasons, can count on at least the possibility of effecting changes in the larger society. Consider, for example, Richard Epstein, Professor of Law at the University of Chicago. Epstein is the author of two books, both of them highly technical and bristling with arguments that would seem to be of interest only to those deeply inside the legal academy; but nevertheless these two studies—*Takings: Private Property and the Power of Eminent Domain* (Cambridge, Mass., 1985) and *Forbidden Grounds: The Case against Employment Discrimination Laws* (Cambridge, Mass., 1992)—are now playing an important role in an attempted restructuring of American society. How and why has this happened?

It has not happened simply because Epstein's arguments are (as he advertises them to be) novel and against the grain of current understandings of the fields of law he treats. Novelty is a requirement of publication in law journals no less than it is for publication in *PMLA* or *Diacritics*, but in neither field does its achievement assure extra-disciplinary effectiveness. Nor has it happened because Epstein's arguments can be mapped directly on to questions of public policy, for this is often true too of literary arguments, especially of the kind new historicists like to make. Rather it has happened because in various corners of our society individuals and groups are searching for ways to pursue certain ends and Epstein belongs to a class of people, law professors, to which anyone interested in effecting immediate change is likely to turn. It is not enough that his reasoning is such that it will appeal to those groups—that might well be the case of a professor of history or English; it is necessary that he be *already* tied into networks of communication and political action whose members are poised to hear his thesis even before it is announced.

That thesis is simple but deeply cutting: traditionally the constitutional prohibition of the taking of private property by the state without just compensation has been read as applying to *direct* takings: for example, the state appropriates my land for the purposes of building a highway, but must make good my loss by paying me cash or providing me with alternative land or some other recompense. Epstein, however, would extend the principle to *indirect* governmental actions that fall short of outright seizure, but nevertheless restrict the use I can make of my property and thereby deprive me of the value that is inseparable from my ownership of it. Two such state actions, according to Epstein, take the form of environmental laws and anti-discrimination laws. I may own land at the shore and find that a law, not directed at me but impacting me, has been passed that forbids the erection of buildings above a certain height; the land is still mine—it hasn't been taken—but its utility to me is greatly diminished and I receive nothing in return except the assurance (which I may not value at all) that it is all to the ecological good. Or I may operate a business and have access to a ready pool of skilled labour, but be told that, according to a new law, I must transform my workforce to make it more representative of the minority populations in my community. Again, the business is still mine, but costs have been added to its operation which have the effect of depriving me of profit that would have been legally (i.e. without fraud or

duress) earned, and the loss has been visited upon me without
recompense of any kind. An expansive view of the just compensation requirement, one that rested on the priority of property
rights to the legislation of community morals or 'quality of life',
would remedy these situations by monetarizing state encroach-
ment even when it is directed at no one in particular.

It would also of course threaten all environmental and anti-
discrimination laws because the state treasury could not possibly
bear the cost of fighting the innumerable claims that would
immediately be filed against it. That is why, despite the declaration that under current law his argument is 'wildly inconceivable'
(*Forbidden Grounds*, 5), that very same argument is now on the lips
of many who couldn't care less about the doctrine of eminent
domain or about the history of constitutional interpretation.
These are (among others) developers, timber companies, manu-
facturers, real estate agents, hunters, large and small employers,
all of whom know a weapon when they see it. They *get* to see it
because as organized interests they have lawyers and lobbyists
whose job it is to come up with innovative strategies that might
offset whatever obstacles have been put in the way of their free
enterprise policies. Epstein's thesis opens the window to just
such a strategy and even as I write causes of action based on his
books are making their way through the courts. The fact that
two of Epstein's colleagues on the Chicago faculty are influential
federal judges who know other federal judges who know . . . (you
get the idea) doesn't hurt.

The point is not that Epstein's influence depends on his political connections, but that the presence or absence of political connections could possibly be a factor in his influence. The influence
of a literary critic, in contrast, will be independent of whether or
not he has friends in high places, unless one of those friends
appoints him to a government position. No revisionary interpretation of a literary text will ever have a public career, even if it
were to be as 'wildly inconceivable' under 'current law' as is
Epstein's assault on anti-discrimination law. Claudius as the hero

of *Hamlet*? Mr Collins as the normative centre of *Pride and Prejudice*? *The Waste Land* as a paean to the felicities of modern life? No less controversial in their way than the expansion of just compensation to include indirect impacts, but unlikely to be the vehicles of a ripple effect that would take the controversy to the halls of Congress or the chambers of the Supreme Court. The moral is clear, and fatal both to the ambitions of the new historicists and to the fears of those who oppose them: no one cares very much about literary criticism outside the confines of its *professional* practice.

To this moral must be attached another: an augmented effectivity for literary–cultural work will not be achieved by changes internal to the profession's practice, even if those changes are made in the name of an expanded sense of the ways in which literary–cultural work is affected by and affects in turn other kinds of work in the society. Even when new historicists alter their interpretive practices so as to reflect the conviction that both the objects of their attention and the forms of that attention are deeply implicated in society-wide structures of power and legitimization, the analyses they produce will not constitute an intervention in those structures. Those analyses will certainly be different—a reading of *Paradise Lost* as a stage in the production of the bourgeois subject is surely different from a reading of *Paradise Lost* as a Christian epic—but that difference will not make a difference of the kind new historicists often claim and desire. The return to literary criticism of political questions does not make literary criticism more political in any active sense.

We can test this thesis by putting it up against an argument made by Donald Pease. Pease is concerned to assess the effects of a shift in the field of American studies from the unselfconscious work of critics who reproduce in their analyses the content of liberal ideology to the very self-conscious work of 'New Americanists' (a term coined in derision by Frederick Crews), who insist on both uncovering that ideology and acknowledging their own inability wholly to escape it. Thus while Henry Nash

Smith in *Virgin Land* largely accepts and represents the politically charged narrative of America's heroic expansion to the west, someone like Richard Slotkin will see in the trope of the virgin land 'an ideological cover-up for Indian removal, frontier violence, government theft, land devastation, class cruelty, racial brutality and misogyny' ('New Americanists: Revisionist Interventions into the Canon', in H. Aram Veeser, ed., *The New Historicism Reader*, New York, 1994, 143). Moreover, Pease continues, in offering this revisionist account, Slotkin does more than put forward a new reading; for he is not merely contesting Smith's interpretation, but asserting that interpretations like Smith's *do work* (the point is the one Williams makes with reference to the standard line on the pastoral), and that the work they do is not located outside the play of ideological forces but within that play and is therefore complicit with those forces. It follows then that the proudest boast of an older American studies—that it is not crudely ideological and political but is, rather, generously capacious in the style mandated by liberal thought—is in fact a sign of its political co-optation and its ideological complicity, a complicity all the more insidious because it is hidden even from itself. If the liberal imagination, in Pease's words, 'represents the denial of political questions', a depoliticized criticism extends that denial, and, correspondingly, a repoliticized criticism does its part to bring those questions to the surface, and, not incidentally, marks the extent to which its own politics are an inescapable component of the story it tells. 'When their work . . . realizes the connection between their disciplinary practices and oppositional political movements, New Americanists separate their discipline from the liberal consensus' (148).

So goes Pease's argument, and I find it not only powerful, but, in its essential features, true. But I become uneasy when he contends that by realizing 'the connection between their disciplinary practices and oppositional political movements', New Americanists undermine 'the separation of the public world from the cultural sphere' (148) and make themselves into a new kind of rational amphibian: 'For as *liaisons between* cultural and public realms, they are at once within the field yet external to it' (158). But if this is true, it is true for everyone, not just for Pease and his friends. The attempt to claim for the New Americanists a superior state of integration with the political world is at odds with the New Americanists' thesis that such integration is inevitable even for those who do not recognize it as their own condition. The Americanists of a previous generation may have thought of themselves as being insulated from the public sphere, but in fact they were as interconnected as anyone else. And by the same token, these benighted consumers and reproducers of the liberal ideology were as much within the field *and* outside it as their enlightened successors. Henry Nash Smith no less than Richard Slotkin was an amphibian, at once an actor within a demarcated space of disciplinary gestures and a citizen of the larger society whose values and priorities underwrote both the intelligibility and the currency (in two senses) of those gestures.

What Pease has done here is confuse two levels of analysis, the theoretical and the material, or rather, he thinks that there is more of a relation between them than I do. The first level is the level of a general truth: all activities in a society are interrelated in ways that render it impossible for the actions taken in any one to be without consequences for the shape of any other. But it is the second level, the level of the material, that largely determines the degree and immediacy of these consequences. That is to say, the present realization of the general truth will depend on the relays of power and influence that are currently in place. It is in relation to those relays or routes and not in relation to the strength of an idea that the impact of one sphere on another will be either immediate or etiolated or something in between. The fact that the New Americanists now think of themselves as participating in a project different from that of their predecessors will not alter the relationship between their analyses and the material conditions they now thematize. Just because a critic ends his reading of *Sister Carrie* or *The Grapes of Wrath* with a discussion of the homeless rather than with an account of literary realism does not mean that his discussion and the proposals it may contain will find their way to the offices of the Department of Housing and Urban Development. While it is certainly true that ideas can change the material world, the configurations of the material world are such that some ideas emanating from some precincts will register more directly than others. A theory can only have the effects allowed to it by the very conditions it would alter.

It follows then that I cannot share in the hope Pease expresses at the end of his essay when he looks forward to what might eventuate from the New Americanists' insistence on linking 'repressed sociopolitical contexts *within* literary works to the sociopolitical issues *external* to the academic field'. 'When they achieve critical mass,' he says, 'these linkages can change the hegemonic self-representation of the United States' culture' (158). The question of course is 'When will that be? When will critical mass be achieved?', and behind that question is the more urgent one, 'By what means will it be achieved?' The answer can not be that the achievement will follow from the mere accumulation of linkages of the New Americanist kind; for, as I have said repeatedly, these linkages themselves have to have something to link up to and a mechanism that is doing the linking and as yet literary academics, New Americanist or any other, have neither and cannot will them into existence.

At times, however, the linkages to the linkages are already in place, waiting for an agenda to take advantage of them; and that is why Pease's central example of New Americanist newness—the shift from a Henry Nash Smith style account of western expansion to a Richard Slotkin-type account—gives some substance to his hopes. For it so happens—it is a matter of *contingent* fact—that the representation of the Frontier adventure has long been an issue of general public concern, and that there has always been a strong connection between the nation's sense of itself and a tradition of academic/cultural description stretching from

Frederick Jackson Turner to Henry Nash Smith. A challenge to that tradition, as opposed to the traditions in which Spenser and Milton have been described, will register in precincts far beyond the academy and, in this instance at least, an alteration in cultural work has a sporting chance of changing 'the hegemonic self-representation of the United States' culture'. When I write that *Lycidas* is not a meditation on the pastoral, but a deep and involuntary expression of Milton's fear of women, only my fellow Miltonists will be either excited or exasperated. But when Richard Slotkin, Annette Kolodny, Jane Tompkins, and Patricia Limerick produce revisionary accounts of western expansion, they challenge more than a scholarly orthodoxy; they challenge a national self-image that has made its way into every corner of American life, and it is no surprise to find their work debated in the op-ed pages of the *New York Times* and *Wall Street Journal* in addition to the pages of more rarified professional journals.

Is there a general lesson to be derived from this example of academic work impacting on the larger society? I think not, unless it is the lesson that anyone who wishes to participate directly in the restructuring of American society should become a New Americanist, and preferably one whose area of scholarly concern is the cultural representation of the West or some other cultural prime—Abraham Lincoln comes to mind—so central to the public imagination that a critique of it is sure to become notorious and controversial. This, however, is a lesson unlikely to be heeded for reasons I have already enumerated. First of all, we do not ordinarily choose to enter a field because it affords an opportunity to be effective in some other; we do not survey the various periods and specializations and ask which of them can best serve as a bridge to spheres of activity far removed from its everyday practice. Rather we become *interested* in something—in an author, a text, a genre, a problem in theory—and it is usually *later*, under the pressure of anxieties created by the demand for justification, that we tell ourselves a story in which the pursuit of our interest is crucial for the improvement of the human condition.

Moreover, even if legions of literary/cultural critics decided to crowd into those few areas of study that looked as if they might be highways to national influence, the material conditions of professional life would not allow it. There wouldn't be enough jobs and there wouldn't be enough bodies to do the other jobs—like teaching Spenser, Pope, and Jane Austen—that would still be required by the institutions that employ us. And even if this difficulty could be overcome, and the institution were somehow persuaded to allow a large number of its spaces to be unoccupied so that everyone or nearly everyone could do the same kind of work, the sameness of that work would soon become a reason no longer to do it; for while it may for a time be the fashion to produce deconstructive analyses of established cultural formations, the tastes within the profession for that fashion will quickly be sated; and presented with still another exposure of the hegemonic force of politically naturalized traditions, people will begin to say, as they are saying even now, 'Oh no, not that tired old number again; give me a break, or, better still, give me a reading of "Dover Beach".'

The fact that for a few years now the profession has taken to interrogating its own procedures with an eye toward discovering (and wallowing in) their impurity does not mean that the profession has now found its true course and discovered what it really wants; for what the profession really wants is the renewal of its energies, a new angle from which to exercise its skills, and when that renewal has become old, as it surely has, the project of interrogating its own procedures will go the way of all other thematizations, honourably or dishonourably retired in favour of the new kid or the re-newed kid on the block. In short, that form of criticism which bills itself as breaking out of the confines of the profession is no more (nor less) than a turn in the professional wheel. The politics that brings politics to the fore is the professional—disciplinary—politics that is ritually (and self-righteously) scorned. I have been arguing that conditions in the larger society prevent it from hearkening to the news from literary and cultural studies; it is also the case that resistance to the linking up of the two spheres comes from literary and cultural studies themselves; that is, from pressures *internal* to a history that brings with it a very particular set of needs and requirements. Despite occasional appearances to the contrary, the conversation that takes place within the humanistic academy and the conversation that leads to legislative and administrative action remain segregated from one another. (And even if they were not segregated but were brought together effectively on some occasion, they would still be distinctive conversations that just happened to interact because of contingent historical circumstances.)

It might seem that the events of the past several years present a powerful counter-example to this moral. As everyone knows, the debates about 'political correctness' and multiculturalism have focused on the humanities, and one bizarre side-effect has been the demonizing of a few professors of English, philosophy, and French who have been declared responsible for disasters of a kind usually attributed to nuclear war or the bubonic plague: the collapse of Western civilization, the triumph of force over reason, etc. Suddenly in the pages of *Time*, *Newsweek*, the *New Republic*, the *Atlantic Monthly*, and in op-ed pieces written for the *Wall Street Journal*, the *New York Times*, the *Washington Post*, the *Los Angeles Times*, the *San Diego Union*, the sins of literary critics are rehearsed for a public whose appetite for anti-academic news seems insatiable. Nor is there any reluctance to name names. Nationally syndicated columnist George Will excoriates new historicist Stephen Greenblatt for reading *The Tempest* as an exploration of the policies and practices of colonialism; Eve Sedgwick is regularly vilified and ridiculed for the title of a piece ('Jane Austen and the Masturbating Girl') none of her detractors has ever read: the person of Paul de Man becomes the occasion for the drawing of a retroactive line between deconstruction and fascism; the beginning of the end is identified with the rise of reader-response criticism, with special (and dismissive) mention of my own *Surprised by Sin*. Surely the wide circulation of such complaints, complete with thumbnail sketches of the offending arguments, constitutes a refutation of the thesis that literary criticism will never enter a national conversation and become the subject of *general* (as opposed to academic) interest.

Not really. In fact the apparent exceptions *prove* my rule because critics who have entered the public consciousness have done so not by virtue of their own efforts or ambitions, but because of the efforts and ambitions of those who have appropriated them as symbols of a threat they do not in fact pose. In an ironic turnabout (which is hardly fair play) the wilder claims of some literary critics—claims of subversion and revolution more grandiose than anything we find in Montrose—are accepted at face value and then paraded as evidence of a conspiracy against which the entire nation is urged to take arms. The object of outrage, it is important to note, is not any of the work literary critics actually do—the painstaking and detailed analysis of texts—but the supposed implications of that work as drawn out by people who have never read it and who therefore, it can be safely said, do not know it. This ignorance, however, is not a handicap because the audience to whom the horror story of academics run amok is retailed does not know it either; consequently, the transaction between them is unimpaired by an obligation to confront the shared target of scorn in the context of its disciplinary productions with its inconvenient history of origins, competing models of practice, and internal debate on every level. Instead one party simply holds up exhibit 1—the game is 'show and tell'—and says, 'Isn't this horrible' (*this* being a cartoon caricature of what really goes on in any classroom), and the other party—made up largely of journalists even more ignorant than those who supply them with materials—responds by crying, 'Yes, yes, off with their heads. Or at least with their jobs.'

Were this another kind of essay I would give a more complete account of recent events, an account that would include the strategy by which a consortium of right-wing think-tanks, foundations, and well-placed individuals (the Secretary of Education, the Chair of the National Endowment for the Humanities, on occasion the President of the United States), with the help of journalists convinced, as they can be at the drop of a hat, that the First Amendment was in danger, saturated the media with a simple story (the story of there being a simple story), largely anecdotal and completely without benefit of research, that became 'true' simply by virtue of its repetition.

The path of this story was smoothed by the absence of anything put in its way. At the very moment when literary critics (or at least a few of them) were finally given the attention they had regarded as their never-to-be-conferred due, it became clear that they were totally unprepared to perform in the spotlight, largely, I think, because the spotlight was not their own. That is, they were not being challenged on their home ground by rival readings of Shakespeare and Spenser; rather the arena was shifted to the theatre of national politics where their work and persons were assigned roles that bore little relationship to the actual facts and actual tasks performed. (I, for example, was mischaracterized as a rabid academic leftist–Marxist, a piece of miscasting that was an insult to all *real* leftists and Marxists.)

As a result, the literary community was immediately put on the defensive, forced to answer the charge that its most prominent members believed that words are meaningless, that values and standards are political impositions, that interpretation is entirely a matter of force and will, that no one's interpretation can be said to be wrong, that there is no rationale for deciding when one work is better than another. (I know of no influential theorists who believe any of these things.) Ill-suited to the rough-and-tumble of public debate, academics could only respond in their own language, a language that was quickly seized upon as still more evidence of their arrogance, solipsism, and irresponsibility. After a period of shell-shock lasting more than six months (October 1990–May 1991), a few counter-voices began to be heard, and, even as I write, full-length refutations are beginning to appear. But the damage had already been done; an image of academic life in general and of literary activity in particular had been put in general circulation where it could be easily exploited for cheap political effect, as it was when Vice President Quayle blamed the country's problems on a cultural élite who hang out in the faculty lounge where, as he imagined it, they sit around plotting the subversion of family values.

Certainly this is notoriety of a kind, but it couldn't be more different from the attention paid to Richard Epstein. In Epstein's case an academic project—the revisionary re-reading of some key concepts in constitutional law—has made its way into the public domain where it is doing real (if, in my mind, regrettable) work. In the case of Stephen Greenblatt or Eve Sedgwick or Paul de Man, an academic project—a revisionary reading of some key concepts in literary interpretation—has been lifted out of the context that provides its intelligibility and turned into an all-purpose scapegoat that can be excoriated without ever having to engage it on its own terms. Literary critics may interpret their new prominence in the popular press as evidence that the larger society now takes them seriously, but in fact it is evidence that the larger society has no interest in them at all except as improbable perpetrators of ills they did not cause and cannot remove. It is precisely because we are so marginal that we can be inflated into a threat no one is really afraid of. Montrose reads an editorial in his local newspaper that attacks new historicism by name and concludes from this attention 'that there is something immediately important at stake in our reading and teaching of Shakespeare' ('Professing the Renaissance', 29). But what is important to the editorial writer is the opportunity to score a political point at the expense of a few professors without the power to fight back. The newspaper's indifference to the way Shakespeare is interpreted is indicated in its characterization of the bard's work as 'deathless prose'. When the honour of an author is defended by someone who seems not to have read him, you can be sure that the gesture is directed not at the critical community but at another audience altogether, the audience of those who resent the academy in part because they know so little about it. Even though literary criticism now occupies a place in the public consciousness that few would have dreamt of three years ago, it is still the case, as I asserted earlier, that no one in the greater world cares one way or the other about literary criticism *as such*, even though for a short time people cared (negatively) about literary criticism as a symbol of something they abhorred. It follows then that no one can reasonably hope or fear that simply by foregrounding such issues as the politics of gender in his readings of Spenser and Shakespeare he can participate in the reformation of twentieth-century culture.

It could be objected that I am reading Montrose too strongly and that the verb 'participate' can be taken in a much softer and less dramatically interventionary sense. That is, 'participate' could mean no more than contribute in a real but unpredictable and contingent way to the formation of attitudes that may in time combine with other changes in discursive and material practice to alter the present arrangement of things. Such a hope, modest in scope, would find confirmation in the experience of every teacher who has ever been told by a former student that something he said or wrote has exerted a lifelong influence, profoundly shaping the performance of a lawyer or a legislator or a stockbroker. Who has not beamed with pleasure at hearing himself credited with such effects, but who has not, at the instant of pleasure, been bemused if not amazed by a career of influence he did not contemplate at the moment of instruction? It may be, as Montrose asserts, that literary criticism, like any other text, 'is socially productive and . . . performs work in the process of being written, enacted or read' (23), but the work it performs at a distance from its home precincts—work that may not show up for years and then in forms so mediated as to be unrecognizable—cannot be what the critic has in mind when he sets about his task.

When I say 'cannot' I do not intend a moral stricture but a practical impossibility: when one sits down to do a literary or a legal job, one's sense of what questions are appropriate to ask, of what answers fall within the range of a shared intelligibility, of what boundaries must be respected and what others might be extended, flows from a focused grasp of the distinctiveness of what one is trying to do, from an awareness, not added to the performance but constitutive of it, that the point of the effort is *this* (to interpret a poem, to argue a case, advocate legislation) and not *that* (anything else). Were that focus to be relaxed, were the agent to substitute for the point of the inquiry the point of some other inquiry by asking, for example, not what does this poem mean, but what will be the effect on foreign policy or on the literacy crisis or on the culture wars of assigning the poem meaning *X*, the practice of literary criticism would not have been given a wider scope or made deeper and more relevant but abandoned. It will not have been abandoned in an unprincipled way, but in the service of principles (and concerns) other than those that animate an act of literary interpretation. You will still say something about the poem that is the putative object of your attention, but what you think to say will not be provoked by a desire to interpret the poem—to get it *right*—but by a desire to *use* it as part of an extra-literary strategy.

In a now forgotten interlude in the history of Milton criticism, *Paradise Lost* was appropriated for the purposes of Allied propaganda. The chief exhibit is G. Wilson Knight's *The Chariot of Wrath: The Message of John Milton to Democracy at War* (London, 1942). The subtitle telegraphs Knight's intention: he is going to search Milton's poetry for passages and images that will provide comfort and inspiration to a nation beleaguered by evil forces; he is *not* going to claim that the meanings he finds are the meanings Milton intended: only that the meanings he finds are helpful to the British people in a moment of present crisis. What follows is an allegorical reading of the epic that presupposes a homology between the battle of Christ against Satan and the battle of Winston Churchill (an excerpt from one of whose addresses graces Knight's title-page) against Hitler, and generates innumerable parallels including a once famous (or infamous) characterization of the onrushing chariot of God in book VI as a 'gigantic, more than human, airplane' (159). On the other side of the Atlantic Douglas Bush was not impressed. While 'One may respect the feeling behind' Knight's allegorization, Bush grumbled, it may nevertheless be thought 'that Milton might have preferred relatively intelligible criticism to a whirlwind apotheosis' (*Paradise Lost in Our Time*, Ithaca, NY, 1945, 6). Bush misses the point. The intelligibility Knight is after is not literary, but topical and political. He wants to rouse a nation; he wants to be a national cheer-leader; and in the context of *those* purposes, details that seem strained and even bizarre to Bush are perfectly apposite. Of course Bush need not have worried. Knight's 'whirlwind apotheosis' is barely remembered and has had no lasting effect on Milton criticism. It could not have had because it was not a critical, but a hortatory, effort and once the occasion provoking it had passed from the scene (once World War II was won) it ceased to be of interest and the tradition returned, with scarcely a ripple, to its former ways.

The example of *The Chariot of Wrath* allows me to underline a point made earlier. It is one thing to say that everything is political when it means no more nor less than that any task one prosecutes proceeds within contestable assumptions; it is another thing to say that the inescapably political nature of disciplinary acts in this sense means that one engages in them with specifically political intentions. Were I to offer a reading of *Paradise Lost*, it could be challenged at any point by someone who believed (and could back up his belief with discipline-specific reasons) that his reading was the better one. Each of us would be proceeding in a controversial manner and therefore each of us would be proceeding politically; but neither of us would be proceeding within a political intention because we would both be possessed by the same desire, to get at the truth about *Paradise Lost*. If that were not our desire, if instead either of us pursued an interpretive direction (itself political in the inescapable and trivial sense) because it furthered a political end—passing a piece of legislation, defeating a particular candidate—he would be acting as a politician and no longer be a literary critic.

A politician is what Knight becomes when he writes *The Chariot of Wrath*, and that is why Bush's critique of the book is wide of the mark. Bush may think that he is quarrelling with Knight's interpretation of *Paradise Lost*, but what he is really quarrelling with is Knight's decision to exchange the project of interpreting *Paradise Lost* for the project of producing immediate political consequences. Knight is not participating in the (then popular) game of arguing about whether Satan is the hero of the poem; rather he is using the vocabulary and materials of that game to play another one, and he had good, extra-literary, reasons for doing so. The difference between the two games emerges when one thinks about what might be an appropriate challenge to his reading. It would not be appropriate to remind him of the history of epic conventions or of the topoi of Renaissance heroism. It would be appropriate (although in 1942 risky) to argue that his contrast between the Axis and Allied powers is too sharply drawn and that after all there is a case to be made for Hitler's actions. Making a case for Hitler would have struck Knight as perverse and wrong-headed; making a case for being faithful to Milton's literary intentions would have struck him as wilfully missing the point of his book, which is to condemn and to cheer, not to explicate. Obversely, we miss the point when the first question we ask of a literary work or of an interpretation of a work is whether or not it furthers the struggle against oppression.

The obvious rejoinder to this is 'Who says?' as in 'Who are you to say what questions we may and may not ask about a literary work; if a sufficient number of persons succeeds in changing the mode of interrogation thought appropriate to literary studies, then literary studies will have a new shape and your strictures will be heard as the dyspeptic complaints of someone whose day has come and gone.' Now it is certainly true that if enough people produce their interpretations with an eye to their immediate political effect (something Knight was at least able to do by virtue of the special circumstances of the war and the status of *Paradise Lost* as a national epic) and call what they do literary criticism then literary criticism will be coextensive with what they do. It is not that it cannot be done (it is done all the time) but that doing it will be attended by losses as well as by gains and it is reasonable to ask whether the one outweighs the other. The gains, we are told, would include the more effective participation of literary intellectuals in the great struggles of political life; but what I have been arguing is that, given the shape of political life in the United States, that gain is unlikely to be achieved without changes of a kind that literary intellectuals are incapable of bringing about. What would be lost, and is already being lost, are the skills of close reading that are identified with, and give a distinctive identity to, the profession of literary studies. New historicists and cultural materialists tell us that if we hearken to them, we will do what we do better. I am saying that if we hearken to them, we will no longer be doing what we do but doing something else, which will be neither better nor worse but different.

One might think that it would be possible to pay a double attention, at one moment doing full justice to the verbal intricacy of a poem and at the next inquiring into the agendas in whose service that intricacy has been put. But here one must recall the difficulty of serving two masters; each will be jealous of the other and demand fidelity to its imperatives. Those new historicists who continue to perform new-critical-style analyses of the texts they study are accused by their colleagues to the left of them (and there is always someone to the left of anybody) of aestheticizing the real-world questions they claim to be raising; those who leave aesthetic issues behind and say nothing at all about the language of their favourite exhibits are accused of having subordinated literary value to a personal agenda. Both sides have a point, although it is not the point either would make. The point is the tautological one that different activities are different and engaging in them will be differently productive. When you exchange one activity for another, you lose something, and although you might mask the loss by calling the new activity by the old name, the phenomena that came into view under the previous dispensation will have disappeared in your brave new world. Maybe they should disappear, maybe the pleasures particular to close literary analysis are too esoteric and over-refined in a time of great social urgency, but we should at least have a clear idea of what would be at stake were we to think of ourselves as politicians first, and literary critics second, if at all.

I would not want to be understood as taking an essentialist position here. I am not saying that there is a fixed entity called 'literary studies' and that those who reject its decorums are committing a crime against the category. In fact it is because literary study is a conventional activity, one shaped by the vocabulary, distinctions, and questions it employs, that it behoves us to be wary of discarding its machinery. If the category were essential rather than conventional, if it named a natural kind rather than an artefact of history, a departure from it by a generation of practitioners would do it no permanent harm; it would still be there waiting to be rediscovered by the faithful. A conventional activity, however, lives and dies by the zeal with which we ask its questions and care about the answers. A conventional activity is one whose possibility and intelligibility depend on a specialized and artificial vocabulary which is generative of the phenomena it picks out, in this case the range of verbal nuances that emerge when one takes up the tools of close reading, semiotics, and poetics. If that vocabulary falls into disuse, the facts it calls into being will no longer be produced or experienced. If no one any longer asks 'What is the structure of this poem?' or 'What is the intention of the author and has it been realized?' or 'In what tradition does the poet enrol himself and with what consequences for that tradition?', something will have passed from the earth and we shall read the words of what was once literary criticism as if they were the remnants of a lost language spoken by alien beings.

====

Looking Elsewhere: Cultural Studies and Interdisciplinarity

I N the course of these lectures I have addressed epistemological questions only glancingly, but it is important, I think, to
get clear on at least one or two points before continuing. As
you will recall, I have several times used the example of the law
as a foil with which to set off certain issues of literary studies. I
pointed out that when a client comes to a lawyer he tells a story
that in his mind has obvious crucial features and decisive
moments; but that when the lawyer hears the story, she hears it
quite differently and with different emphases; indeed what may
appear most significant to the client may drop out altogether in
her considerations of the matter, for what she has been doing is
translating—one might even say transubstantiating—what is told
her into the appropriate *legal* categories, into the categories that
will allow her to determine whether or not the client has a *legal*
cause of action.

There is a temptation to regard what happens in this process
as a distortion of reality by the special vocabulary of a mere discipline, and as a cautionary tale as to why one should not put
oneself into the hands of lawyers. This was the mistake made *en
masse* by American Legal Realists, who believed that if they could
only get rid of the machinery of the legal culture—with its terms
of art, constructed entities, and artificial rules—they would be
closer to seeing what was *really* going on when someone was in
search of a legal remedy. But it is my contention that if you were

to get rid of the machinery of the legal culture (or of the literary culture, or of the anthropological culture) you would not be improving the law, you would be replacing the law with the machinery of some other discipline, with *its* specialized vocabulary, normative distinctions, taxonomies, articulations, etc. You might in fact decide to do just that—abandon law and the possibility of a *legal* remedy for some other enterprise—but it should be clear, as it was not to the Legal Realists, that it is that you were doing, and not engaging in the effort of reform.

The point has been well made by Mark Cousins, who says that in the law 'really' is used in a specialized sense. ' "Really" is what is relevant to the law, what is definable by law, what may be argued in terms of law and evidence, what may be judged and what may be subject to appeal' in legal terms (*Post Structuralism and the Question of History*, Cambridge, 1987, 132–3). I want to say that 'really' is always used in just such a specialized sense, that is, in a sense that acquires its intelligibility in relation to some elaborated enterprise or discipline; and, moreover, that this isn't the dreaded Relativism or some other supposedly post-structuralist horror, because in a world where the ultimate grounds of reality are not available to us even as we live them out—in our world as opposed to the world as seen by God—the facts and values and opportunities for action delivered to us by various discursive formations are not second-hand, are not illusions, are not hegemonic impositions, but are, first of all, the best we have, and, second, more often than not adequate to the job. The job, in my argument, will of course always be a particular one, a job of history, or of law or of literary criticism or of whatever; and these different jobs will be just that, *different*, and not in themselves capable of being ranked as closer or more removed from the master job of describing reality as it really is. (Ranking is, of course, something that happens; in our culture science is usually thought to have the job of describing reality as it really is; but its possession of that franchise, which it wrested away from religion, is a historical achievement not a natural right.) Jobs are useful and appropriate for *purposes* and what is good for one purpose may not be so for another.

Taken to its conclusion, this line of reasoning has two casualties. The first is the attempt to elevate some job or discipline above others on the grounds that it is more in touch with the *Ding an Sich*. In recent years this attempt has taken the form of privileging historicist work over literary work or of announcing (it amounts to the same thing) that only if literary work is resolutely historical is it worthy of our attention. But if I am right, historical work is neither superior to, nor the real content of, literary work; it is just a different kind of work. (More of this later.) The second casualty of my argument is the hope that we can put all the jobs of work—all the so-called disciplines—together and form one large and unified field of knowledge (call it cultural studies) to replace the fractured and fragmented knowledges now given us by separate departments and schools. This is the hope of interdisciplinary studies when it becomes a religion— when it becomes an agenda called 'interdisciplinarity'—and it is dashed when one realizes that different forms of disciplinary work, rather than being co-partners in a single teleological and utopian task, are engaged in performing the particular tasks that would pass away from the earth were they to lose themselves in the name of some grand synthesis, be it the discipline of all disciplines or the truth of all lesser and partial truths.

Now it might seem that in making these statements I risk undermining the very arguments I urged on you earlier. How can I come out against the dream of a unified field of knowledge and still refer blithely to the unity and immanent intelligibility of disciplines? How can I deny unity as a hope and assume unity as a given when I come to talk of literary or legal studies? If I were to take seriously the remarks I have just made, wouldn't I extend them to the disciplines I seem to have reified, and acknowledge, as so many have been urging us to do recently, that disciplines are ephemeral, barely existing entities, transitory, shifting, permeable in their boundaries, riven by internal conflict, and in some sense *unreal* since they are but the epiphenomena of larger structural movements which give them whatever borrowed and spurious autonomy they may seem to have?

That is the going wisdom these days and a recently published volume, *Knowledges: Historical and Critical Studies in Disciplinarity* (ed. E. Messer-Davidow, D. R. Shumway, and D. J. Sylvan, Charlottesville, Va., 1993), retails that wisdom in spades. The editors tell us in the introduction that 'disciplines are such by virtue of a historically contingent, adventitious coherence of dispersed elements', and therefore in studying them one 'problematizes their very existence' (3). Three professors of economics declare that disciplines are 'in the process of always becoming other, of multiplying, of undoing their own limits, of fracturing, and even of collapsing'; 'a discipline . . . is . . . always a transitory thing' (151). And a student of disciplines, that is, someone whose disciplinary subject is disciplines, says, 'The ramifications of disciplinary practices . . . are often contradictory and complex rather than coherent, the contending visions of theory and practice disparate rather than merging into . . . unity' (205–6).

To all of which *I* say, 'So what?' The fact that a self-advertised unity is really a grab-bag of disparate elements held together by the conceptual equivalent of chicken-wire, or by shifting political and economic alliances, or by a desire to control the production and dissemination of knowledge, does not make the unity disappear; it merely shows what the unity is made of, not that it isn't one. Just because the unity is underwritten by rhetoric rather than by nature or logic in no way lessens the force of its operation in the moments of its existence. So long as it is even temporarily established, the unity of a discipline has a material existence and therefore has material effects that no analysis can dispel. To think otherwise, to think that by exposing the leaks in a system you fatally wound it, is to engage in a strange kind of deconstructive Platonism—strange because Platonism is what deconstruction pushes against—in which the surface features of life are declared illusory in relation to a deep underlying truth or non-truth. It is in the surfaces, however, that we live and move and have our being (it is surfaces all the way down) and no philosophical demonstration of their ephemerality will loosen their hold. Even though disciplinary differences are social constructions and, as constructions, infinitely revisable in principle, they nevertheless have force, and it remains true, so long as they *are* in force, that trying to figure out what a poem means will be quite another activity from trying to figure out which interpretation of a poem will contribute to the war effort or to the toppling of patriarchy.

Until recently the assertion of disciplinary difference would have been superfluous, but in some quarters it is now regarded as problematic or even as flatly wrong, in part because it has come to be an article of faith that the idea of a distinctively literary system of facts and values is at best an illusion and at worst an imposition by the powers that be of an orthodoxy designed to suppress dissent. (This it does, we are told, by encoding its own presuppositions in a set of texts that is then presented as the product of a neutral aesthetic order.)

This conclusion follows from an argument I have myself made in these lectures: neither the form nor the content of a discipline are self-generated, but become perspicuous by virtue of relationships (of similarity and difference) with other disciplines that are themselves relationally, not essentially, constituted. If literature, under most post-Romantic understandings, occupies (has title to) the realm of the 'imagination' it is because other enterprises—law, sociology, chemistry, and engineering would be interestingly different candidates—find their self-understanding (and their methodologies) in a renunciation (not a negative, but an enabling, gesture) of that realm; and each of these enterprises will in turn gain a franchise by pushing away as beside *its* point responsibilities and concerns that 'belong' elsewhere. What this means is that what we do 'here', in our shop, is a function of what they, workers in other shops, do 'over there'; the identity of an activity, that which enables you to know it when you see it, is radically dependent on everything from which it would be distinguished; what appears will be a function of what does not appear. One sees a poem or a tort, but the immediacy of the perception is produced by a stage-setting—by the behind-the-scenes network of interdependent and mutually defining practices—which at once escapes our attention and determines its content. (We don't see 'it', but what 'it' enables us to see.)

As I have already indicated, I am persuaded by this argument, but I dissent from the conclusion often drawn from it, the conclusion that because the grounds of a discipline's possibility exist elsewhere than in its internal workings, you should ignore or bracket those workings when you want to understand the discipline's operation. Just because you can inquire into the conditions which made possible a disciplinary space does not mean that you will best be able to understand what goes on in that (admittedly socially constructed) space by looking outside it. Philosophy and theology acquired the shapes they now have when a single conceptual territory splintered in two, creating separate enterprises authorized to ask and answer different questions; and while this is an important point for someone who wants to understand how the categories, vocabulary, and routine procedures of the two disciplines came into being, you will not get a truer picture of either by setting aside its categories and vocabulary in favour of the history that produced them. The fact that something has been historically constituted should be taken *seriously* by stressing the 'constituted'—it is now (at least for a while) what it is—rather than the 'historically'.

In short it is a mistake to believe that because disciplinary intelligibility finally is a function of what exceeds and escapes it—of what it cannot contain—you can get a better purchase on that intelligibility by looking beyond it. (This is a version of the mistake of thinking that a unity made up of disparate and shifting elements is not a unity.) Yet this is the mistake made again and again in almost every piece of 'high' theory published in recent years. Terry Eagleton insists that 'the literary text bears the impress of its historical mode of production as surely as any product secretes in its form and materials the fashion of its making' (*Criticism and Ideology*, London, 1976, 48). Tony Bennett draws the moral (without endorsing it): 'Rescued from the status of a contingent context or backdrop, what was defined as outside literature has been imported to the very centre of its inside; what seemed circumstantial has been redefined as constitutive' (*Outside Literature*, London, 1990, 282). John Frow provides a gloss: 'the concept of the relative autonomy of the literary system must be understood as the result of particular historical conditions and a particular articulation with other systems, not as an inherent quality of literary discourse' (*Marxism and Literary History*, Cambridge, Mass., 1986, 84). Frow also identifies the methodological consequence (he is at the moment explicating Foucault): 'To analyze a discursive formation is to take as object the conditions of existence of discourse and the conditions of its effectivity' (214). And Robert Scholes articulates the programme: we must 'make the object of study the whole intertextual system of relations that connects one text to others . . . the matrix or master code that the literary text both depends upon and modifies'; if we are 'to teach the interpretation of a literary text, we must be prepared to teach the cultural text as well' (*Textual Power*, New Haven, 1985, 31, 33).

The rewards of making this shift, according to some commentators, will be far greater than a mere gain in literary insight, for the hegemony of academic disciplines operates not only to obscure our view of the objects of our analytical attention, but to obscure our view of the forces that oppress us and prevent us from being truly free. 'Specialized academic disciplines', Ben Agger complains, contribute to 'overall domination by refusing a view of totality desperately needed in this stage of world capitalism, sexism and racism' (*Cultural Studies as Critical Theory*, London, 1992, 17). Since 'the fragmentation and specialization of knowledge leads to its hierarchization', academic disciplines are complicit in 'the reproduction of historical domination' (18); and if we commit ourselves to the project of seeing through these false hierarchies and compartmentalizations, 'we can better recognize the texts counseling our conformity and consumerism for what they are and challenge them' (183).

The name of this project is cultural studies and the promise it offers is well presented in Patrick Brantlinger's *Crusoe's Footprints* (New York, 1990). Cultural studies, he explains, 'aims to overcome the disabling fragmentation of knowledge within the disciplinary structure of the university, and . . . also to overcome the fragmentation and alienation in the larger society which that structure mirrors' (16). As a practice it is therefore 'counter-disciplinary' (24), resisting 'the disciplinary narrowings and specializings' which stand in the way of constructing 'a unified map of knowledge' (72). Cultural studies, in this account, refuses the move by which academic critics keep literature 'separate from all other forms of discourse', insisting that literature is not a 'system', but an 'ensemble', a 'leaky category' that includes 'all other forms of discourse that are supposedly nonliterary'; it has no properties of its own; 'its properties are the properties of discourse in general' (15). Therefore, to understand or explain it, you must look away from it to discourse in general; you must look elsewhere, and that is what cultural studies does, surfacing 'the missing, the ungiven, the underrepresented, the stereotyped, the invisible' (64). Cultural studies, Brantlinger tells us, 'begins with the realization that reading the isolated "classic" or "great book" is not possible without also reading the larger "cultural text" into which it fits' (22).

On its face the logic of this is clear and seems to be compelling: if the literary text emerges in a space and with an effectivity provided by the larger culture, focusing on the larger culture is the way to focus on it. But the logic is flawed in two related directions. First of all, you cannot focus on the background array of social practices, on the 'whole intertextual system of relations' within which everything is interdependent ('heteroglot') and nothing free-standing, without turning it into an object which is itself in need of the kind of explanation it supposedly provides. If the thesis is that what is seen is the precipitate of what is not, then surfacing underlying structures will result only in the institution of a *new* relationship between the 'seen' and its hidden cause, a relationship in which the *previously* hidden cause is now in the position of that which has been made visible and some other hidden cause is presumed to lie below *it*. If knowledge cannot grasp the grounds of its own possibility, producing a new account of those grounds will merely be to produce another surface-masquerading-as-depth that will require unmasking in its turn. In the words of Derrida, 'the trace is never as it is in the presentation of itself. It erases itself in presenting itself' ('Difference', in H. Adams and L. Searle, eds., *Cultural Theory since 1965*, Gainesville, Fla., 1986, 133).

Still, one might say, even if cultural studies must fail of its aspiration to reveal the deep causal structure of things, it *can* do something; it can produce a new object, another text. But that text—what Brantlinger calls the cultural text—has no epistemological or ontological superiority over the texts (of literature, history, law, etc.) it displaces. That is, it is not a larger text or a more inclusive text; it is just a *different* text, with its own emphases, details, and meanings which 'naturally' crowd out the emphases, details, and meanings of other texts. The cultural text, if it comes into view, will not provide a deeper apprehension of the literary text or the legal text; rather it will erase them even in the act of referring to them, for the references will always be produced from *its* angle of interest, not theirs. If cultural studies tells us to look elsewhere to find the meaning of the literary text, I say that if you look elsewhere, you will see something else. Literature, as Tony Bennett observes, 'is not something whose social underpinnings must be sought elsewhere; it *is* a set of social conditions and its analysis consists in identifying the effects of these conditions' (*Outside Literature*, 284).

Bennett's point is a version of the one I have made so many times: a practice only acquires identity (diacritical, not essential, but identity nevertheless) by not being other practices, by presenting itself not as doing everything but as doing one thing in such a way as to have society look to it for specific performance. When the diacritically marked outline of a practice is blurred by a map that brings into relief its affiliations (borrowings, lendings, overlappings) with other practices, those affiliations rather than anything specific to the practice are what become visible. It is just like what happens when a map produced by an automobile association displays the distance between cities; the cities themselves become mere nodes, junctures in a relay, while all the attention is focused on what goes on between them. Looking at such a map one has no sense of the shape, extent, or geography of the cities (it is even worse for the states, which simply disappear), for they are points marking the beginning or end of a journey. In the same way an interdisciplinary map, a map of the routes going in and out of particular disciplines, will not indicate just why any particular discipline is *there*, what it *does*, why anyone takes it seriously. To say this is not to fault the map; its job is to display interconnections rather than interior landscapes; my point is that in doing its job it necessarily fails to do others; in doing justice to the relationships *between* disciplines it slights the immanent intelligibility of disciplines.

In response, one might say as Agger and others do that the immanent intelligibility of disciplines is an illusion and that its status as illusion is what the interdisciplinary map—the limning out of the cultural text—makes clear. But this is to assume that the interdisciplinary map provides a metaphysically superior perspective in the light of which any or all things can be better viewed, as opposed to a *different* perspective in the light of which something can be viewed that could not have been viewed from some other angle. I do not mean by the word 'angle' to suggest a partial opening on a full reality that would be the sum of all angles. An angle is not an open window, but a mould; it does not bring light to an antecedently existing reality, but *form* to a reality that fades when it is replaced by another. Although the interdisciplinary map is general, surveying many disciplines rather than focusing on one, its generality is itself particular, for the shapes it makes available gain their prominence at the expense of the other shapes it renders invisible. The fact that the cultural text has no place in it for the routines and imperatives of specific practices is a sign not of its completeness or deeper perspicuity, but of its partiality. Of course not all partialities are the same except in the sense that they are similarly partial. One could always argue, and argue persuasively, that for a particular purpose at a particular time the partiality of the cultural text will be more helpful than the partiality called literary criticism or philosophy or art history. To say that the cultural text is partial is not to criticize it or to deny its usefulness in certain circumstances; it is merely to deny its claim to be representationally superior to other partial texts that are doing other jobs.

Were it not partial, were the cultural text or interdisciplinary map wholly adequate to every detail in the universe as seen from every possible angle, no one could read it. A text that was adequate to every detail as seen from every possible angle would be unsituated; it would not proceed from a perspective—a 'here not there'—but from everywhere and therefore from nowhere. Human beings, however, cannot be in such a condition of dispersion. Human beings are always in a particular place; that is what it means to be human; to be limited by what a specific coordinate of space and time permits us to see until we move on to another coordinate with its equally (if differently) limited permission. For human beings the formula 'as far as I can see' is more than a ritual acknowledgement of fallibility; it is an accurate statement of our horizon-bound condition; of the fact that at any one moment, the scope of our understanding and, within that understanding, the range of actions we might think to take, are finite and cannot be expanded by an act of will. We do not wake up in the morning and announce as our programme for the day 'I will now see beyond my horizons'.

Not only can human beings not be everywhere; they cannot

be in more than one place, at least not at the same time; and that is why (to circle back to the beginning of this discussion) there is a great difference between trying to figure out what a poem means and trying to figure out which interpretation of a poem will best contribute to the war effort. Each effort only makes sense in relation to the traditions, goals, obligatory routines, and normative procedures that comprise its history and are the content of its distinctiveness; as tasks geared to different purposes, they call on entirely different skills and set in motion different orders of attention. If, for example, I am interested in the moral structure of *Paradise Lost*, I will look at Satan's speeches to see whether or not they display contradiction, evasions, self-deceptions, and hollow posturings; but if I am interested in rousing my troops or rousing a nation I will accept those same speeches (no longer the same) at face value and quarry from them shamelessly so long as they lend themselves to my cause. I cannot, however, do both—perform *as* a literary critic and perform *as* political or military leader—simultaneously; for while the two performances will at some level share *Paradise Lost*, the *Paradise Lost* that emerges at the conclusion of one project will have very little resemblance to the *Paradise Lost* that emerges at the end of the other. Even though the 'same lines' are the material of the two efforts, they are really not the same in any strong sense because the purposes within which they are seen, and by being seen, configured, are entirely different. To be sure, this would not be so in societies like Maoist China or Hitler's Germany where, for a while, literary and political purposes were, by fiat, interchangeable; but this would not mean that in those societies the essential identity of literature and politics was fully revealed, only that through the exercise of power the distinctive concerns of one project had been entirely submerged in the concerns of another. Literary work, like any other, can always surrender its distinctiveness to a political agenda, but when it does, it has not found its true form; it has lost the form that gave it distinctive life.

The point can be generalized: whenever there is an apparent *rapprochement* or relationship of co-operation between projects, it will be the case either that one is anxiously trading on the prestige and vocabulary of the other or that one has swallowed the other; and this will be true not only when one project is academic and the other political, but when both are housed in the academy, perhaps in the same building. Many years ago Douglas Bush and Cleanth Brooks engaged in a celebrated debate, with Bush representing the historical method and Brooks representing what was then, in fact, the New Criticism. At one point Brooks made what appeared to be a conciliatory statement: 'I say again that the literary historian and the critic need to work together and that the ideal case is that in which both functions are united in one and the same man' ('Marvell's "Horatian Ode"', in W. R. Keast, ed., *Seventeenth Century English Poetry: Modern Essays in Criticism*, London, 1962, 355). Now this could be read either as an assertion of the complementarity of the two functions—each supplements the contribution of the other to a single unified task—or as an assertion of the usefulness of historical information to the critic as he goes about his business. If Brooks means the first, he is an early prophet of interdisciplinary studies, which have always been impelled by a desire for 'a unified science, general knowledge, synthesis and the integration of knowledge' (Julie T. Klein, *Interdisciplinarity: History, Theory, Practice*, Detroit, 1989, 19); in the interdisciplinary vision there is only one job to which the various disciplines contribute, each filling in the part of the puzzle assigned to it. But in the alternative reading of Brooks's statement each discipline has its own job, a job that is literally inconceivable apart from its vocabulary, and when one discipline borrows from another—as the critic might borrow from the historian—the borrowed material is instantaneously transformed into grist for the appropriator's mill. This, as it turns out, is Brooks's view of the matter. The question of a poem's organization, he says, 'addresses itself properly to the critic. The historical scholars have not answered it, for it is a question which cannot be answered in terms of historical evidence' (325). Or even more strongly: a 'poem has to be read as a poem . . . what it "says" is a question for the critic to answer, and . . . no amount of historical evidence *as such* can finally determine what the poem says' (339). 'This is not to say', he adds, 'that the same man may not be both historical scholar and critic,' but such a man would be exercising two talents at discreet times rather than combining them in ways that respected the integrity of each.

Many years later Robert Hodge comes to the same (for him unhappy) conclusion. In the course of surveying recent work on the prose and poetry of John Donne, Hodge finds that despite the declared intentions of several authors to marry the disciplines of literature and history, the marriage is never consummated because 'each has a different defining object, which cannot be incorporated into the other domain without challenging the identity of the discipline itself' (*Literature as Discourse*, Baltimore, 1990, 225). Hodge cites as an example Terry Sherwood's book on Donne's thought (*Fulfilling the Circle*, Toronto, 1984), and observes ruefully that while Sherwood may make 'many references to historians of religious thought', these historians 'would have no reason to return the compliment, since . . . he uses [them] to explain an object which is outside their system: the works of a poet' (*Literature as Discourse*, 221). For Sherwood as for the other critics Hodge examines 'explanation goes in one direction' only, and when all is said and done 'the disciplinary boundaries . . . remain in place' (222). This holds too when it is historians who bring literary texts into their narratives; their 'aim is not to illuminate these texts, but to use them to illuminate another object, an object of historical discourse: patterns of family life [or] claims about a revolution in sentiment' (224).

Hodge's analysis of this resistance to merger is right on target. The 'separate developments and histories and the different logonomic rules that organize each as a distinct "discipline" are potent social facts, not to be ignored in the name of an illusory project of unity' (233). And yet no sooner has he said this than he

[84]

issues a call for just such a project: 'The need is . . . to replace the tunnel vision of the past . . . with a broadly based practice that is situated socially and historically' (233). A 'broadly based' practice would be a practice not confined to what Brantlinger derisively terms 'institutional disciplinary narrowings and specializings', narrowings and specializings that are obstacles in the way of a clearer vision; but by the evidence Hodge himself marshals, vision is always specific to exactly those narrowings and specializings in the absence of which we would not have a more adequate perception, but no perception at all. The vocabularies of disciplines are not external to their objects, but constitutive of them. Discard them in favour of the vocabulary of another discipline, and you will lose the object that only they call into being. If a literary critic were to internalize the goals and assumptions of historians in the course of explicating a poem, the result would be an explication that bore none of the marks of literary criticism and a piece of language that would no longer be recognizable as a poem because the vocabulary of description would contain no resources for bringing to light (a phrase weaker than the actual effect) poetic features. And if, conversely, the records of a historical event were read (as it is now fashionable to do) with an eye toward highlighting metaphoric effects, narrative strategies, and the affective sources of so-called evidence, the result would be a semiotic object to which it would seem inappropriate to put the basic historical question: what happened? 'What happened?' is the counterpart in historical studies of the question 'What is it about?' in literary studies; and in both cases, if you slide off the defining question and ask another, you will no longer be doing the same job. What Hodge calls the 'potent social facts' of disciplinary organization are more potent than he knows, for they give us the only leverage and potency we could possibly have; independently of them we would have nothing to say and nothing to do.

The conclusion (resisted by many) is that the effects of one's actions will be largely confined to their disciplinary settings even when those settings receive some grandiose new name like cultural studies. Even as I draw this conclusion I can think of at least three forms of academic study that would seem to constitute a challenge to it: feminism, black studies, and gay and lesbian studies. Surely the effects of feminism extend far beyond the academy's precincts and surely feminists who actively work in the public sphere make use of arguments and slogans developed and elaborated in the classroom and in learned articles. Just as surely the recovery by black studies proponents of forgotten or marginalized African-American writers with the attendant construction of a 'suppressed cultural tradition' has led to, among other things, the arguments of Afrocentrism and the altering of course content and curricula on every level of education; and surely one sees every day the effects of the coalition between gay and lesbian academics and the activist members (often academics themselves) of groups like Queer Nation and Act Up, groups whose activities have placed considerable and effective pressure on legislatures, school boards, corporations, and government departments.

No one could deny this evidence, but one can ask what is it evidence of? It is not, I would contend, evidence that academic work can ripple out to effect changes in the larger society, but that, rather, when changes in the larger society are already occurring, academic work can be linked up to them by agents who find the formulations of that work politically useful. It is a question of the direction of force. Unlike the new historicism and cultural studies, feminism, gay rights activism, and the civil rights movement did not originate in the academy, and academic versions of them acquire whatever extra academic influence they may have by virtue of something already in place in public life; academic feminism, academic gay rights studies, and academic black studies do not cause something but piggy-back on its prior existence. It is no accident that when John Beverley looks for examples of academic work that comes 'into direct relation with the forms of political agency' (*Against Literature*, Minneapolis, 1993, 18), he finds Catherine MacKinnon and Anita Hill, two persons whose political activities precede and give resonance to their academic performances, and not the other way around. It is only because MacKinnon and Hill (and here one might add Edward Said) do political work *already* that they can be paraded as academics with political effectivity. They can hardly be role models for young professors unless one thinks that the list of career options includes drafting (unsuccessful) anti-pornography ordinances or appearing before the Senate judiciary committee on national television or becoming a member of the PLO shadow government.

But, one might object, who is to say what is and is not academic work? Well, it is certainly true that what is and is not academic work is not for me to say or for you either. But the discipline can and does say; for if MacKinnon or Hill were to offer to a committee charged with assessing academic credentials the evidence of their political engagement, they would be told, 'That's all very nice and certainly speaks to your performance as citizens, but it does not speak to what concerns us here.' But that's just the trouble, a persistent questioner might insist: shouldn't we be enlarging the criteria so that more things will count as academic work and academic work will look like, and touch, more things? But if the category of 'academic work' were enlarged to the point that it included almost anything an academic did—whether in the classroom, the jury box, or the town hall—the category would have no content because it would contain everything. When all is said and done, I stand by my conclusion that disciplinary actions issue from narrowly defined disciplinary intentions and can only reasonably (one must leave room for accident and serendipity) aim for disciplinary effects.

This conclusion will be distressing to many because it is subversive of the wish that lives in the hearts of literary academics, the wish to be consequential in ways larger than those made available by the discipline as it is practised every day in classrooms before young men and young women likely to be indifferent, or in journals whose audience is limited to the other 300 people in the world who care whether or not Satan is the real hero of *Paradise Lost*. To some extent this unhappiness at having a less than major role in public affairs can be traced to the general assumption on the part of academics that they are a superior breed. As Brian McCrea recently put it (with no little irony), 'Who among us does not know that he or she is a smarter and better person than any Washington insider . . . ?' (*Addison and Steele are Dead*, Newark, Del, 1990, 208). With considerably less irony, indeed with no irony at all, two well-known historians, Richard E. Neustadt and Ernest R. May, co-authored an entire book (*Thinking in Time: The Uses of History for Decision Makers*, New York, 1986) premised on that rhetorical question and its (to them) obvious answer. Their method is to reconsider policy crises of the past and to analyse the thinking of those responsible for major decisions, especially decisions that turned out badly. Inevitably the fatal flaw in that thinking turns out to be a failure to analogize the present situation to its appropriate historical predecessor. The confused President or Prime Minister or Secretary of State, instead of seeing his alternatives, as he should have, in the light of what Grant did in the battle of X, saw himself as another Bismarck or Napoleon or Alexander. Naturally, the result was disaster, and of course the disaster could have been averted and turned into a triumph if the hapless statesman had been a better historian, or, more to the point, if he had been either Neustadt or May. (I heard an interesting variation on this theme on National Public Radio when one James Banner proposed a 'history watch', an 'instant response' team that would be on the look-out for false historical analogies and illegitimately drawn conclusions as they proceeded from the mouths of politicians and popped up in the daily media. Presumably, this team, no doubt headed by Banner, would do the job Neustadt and May are trying to do—make sure we all get it right—but would do it better.)

The megalomania of this extraordinary thesis—it approaches

insanity—should not obscure the fact that it is only an extreme version of the quite ordinary tendency to believe that the skills attending one's own practice are indispensable for any and all practices. Each discipline wants to label itself 'Good For All Ills' in the manner of the elixirs sold at country fairs by quack doctors. At least one discipline has at times nearly pulled it off. Philosophy has often managed to convince workers in other fields that whatever abilities may apparently be required to excel at a particular task, the true ability, underlying all others, is philosophical. Basically the assertion is that philosophy is not a discipline—a particular angled project—but a natural kind, that it is another name for clear thinking and as such no less relevant to the task, say, of shoemaking than to the task of explicating Kant. In recent years this self-description has persuaded fewer in the academy than it once did, but philosophers (quite sensibly) have found themselves an alternative market and now offer themselves under the name of 'ethicists' to hospitals and other institutions faced with difficult decisions involving matters of life and death. There is an apparent logic to this new employment: surely those who spend their days and nights reflecting on moral dilemmas are the best persons to advise those who are confronted with them. But consider the form such reflection usually takes: you are the engineer of a train and at a certain point the track forks into two branches: if you take the branch to the left you will hit a stalled bus full of schoolchildren; if you take the branch to the right you will hit a stalled car. The car has only one occupant, but it is Saul Bellow, or Madonna, or Michael Jordan, or Margaret Thatcher. What do you do? I submit that if you are seeking counsel at a crucial moment of decision the last person you want to turn to is someone who spends his time thinking up hypotheticals like this one so that he can amaze students with his subtlety.

It is not that subtlety is unwanted when medical or legal issues hang in the balance; it is just that subtlety itself is situation-specific and its various forms do not travel well when they are transported from their (institutionally) natural habitat. When the pinch comes you want to entrust yourself to someone who knows the territory—whether the territory be the hospital room or the boardroom or the locker-room—to someone whose ways of processing information have emerged in the course of long hands-on experience rather than from the brains of self-anointed philosopher-kings.

The argument is even more self-evident when the claimants to universal competence are literary critics. One knows the source of the claim: it follows from the traditional exaltation of literature and especially of poetry as a discourse transcending local contexts. If literature, as Arnold famously declared, is a repository of the best that has been thought and said, it is the best for all times and not merely for its time; and if literature is infused with so general a wisdom, does it not follow that those who are responsible for conveying the literary treasure to the rest of us are similarly wise? The answer is 'no' and no for the same reasons that deny the crown to philosophers. Literary critics do not traffic in wisdom, but in metrics, narrative structures, double, triple, and quadruple meanings, recondite allusions, unity in the midst of apparent fragmentation, fragmentation despite surface unity, reversals, convergences, mirror images, hidden arguments, climaxes, denouements, stylistic registers, personae. This list goes on and on, but it does not include arms control or city management or bridge-building or judicial expertise or a thousand other things, even though many of those things find their way into the texts critics study as 'topics' or 'themes'. While it is true that a critic can exercise his or her bag of tricks on any material whatsoever—on politics, war, science, religion—this does not make him or her an expert in the fields from which those materials are quarried.

I am not saying that specifically literary skills cannot be applied to extra-literary contexts, just that those contexts will remain unaffected by the application. The rhetorical analysis of diplomatic communiqués, political statements, legal documents, presidential addresses, advertising, popular culture, television news, billboards, restaurant menus, movie marquees, and almost anything else one can think of has been an industry for a long time, but in almost no case have State Department officials or the members of the judiciary or even the publishers of Harlequin romances changed their way of doing things as a result of having read—if any of them ever did read—a brilliantly intricate deconstruction of their practices. Think about it. You are about to open a new business or introduce a bill in Congress or initiate an advertising campaign, but you pause to ask yourself, 'What would the readers of *Diacritics* say?' While Terry Eagleton is surely right to observe that 'discourses . . . of all kinds, from film and television to fiction and the languages of natural science, produce effects . . . which are closely related to the maintenance or transformation of our existing systems of power' (*Literary Theory*, Oxford, 1983, 210), those systems will not be altered simply because the signifying practices underlying them have been described in detail by someone whose audience is made up of those who value that kind of work because they do it too.

McCrea pokes some gentle fun at an issue of *Diacritics* in which Derrida and others discuss the threat of nuclear war. He concedes that literary theorists have every right 'to worry about nuclear war' but admonishes them to realize that 'their worries will not reach any larger public because their theories, indeed their vocabularies, are private and subversive rather than common and normative' (251). This is not quite right: the vocabularies of literary theorists are no more private than any others; it is just that the public for whom they are intelligible is small and limited to academic circles within academic circles. In those circles these vocabularies are perfectly normative—their use is a requirement for entry—and constitute a common and immediately convertible currency; but these norms and currencies do not authorize or buy anything in other circles where equally public vocabularies are the officially recognized mediums of exchange. In relation to a strongly enforced territoriality, the language of literary theory is not subversive, but irrelevant: *it cannot be heard* except as the alien murmurings of a galaxy far away.

[91]

Then why traffic in it? Why should anyone *do* this kind of work if, as I have said, it is of interest by and large only to those few others who do it too? What's the pay-off? What's the justification? How do we respond when we are asked or ask ourselves, 'Why *this*, and not something else, building bridges, saving lives, fixing toilets?' These are of course the questions that have always lain just below the surface of everything I have been saying, and if you want the answers—or at least *my* answer—you will have to come back yet once more.

Why Literary Criticism Is
Like Virtue

ONE of the pleasures of giving these lectures, over and above the general pleasures of being in Oxford, has been a number of chance meetings with members of the audience who pause on the street or in a café or in a book-shop to say hello and ask a question, usually in the form of a mild (at least in tone) objection. One of you (Professor Avraham Oz) even took the time to send me a substantial letter, in which the main thesis of these lectures—that academic work is one thing and political work another—was strongly contested. Let me share with you some of the letter-writer's points and my replies.

His first point, which he acknowledged is in no way in conflict with what I have been saying, is that, as an Israeli, he inhabits a culture where the relationship between academic productions and political acts is much closer than in the United States; indeed, given the fact that in his country some of the leading literary intellectuals have also been among the nation's most prominent politicians, it is inevitable that those who perform and consume exegetical labours do so with a strong sense of the potential con-nection between them and the urgent questions of the day; and this holds true when the text being explicated is Shakespeare, and especially true if it is *The Merchant of Venice*.

As he and I agree, however, this coincidence of the literary and the political contexts is not generalizable since it flows from the particular fact of a society in which being Jewish, being a citizen, being a patriot, and being a cultural critic are all bound up with one another. Moreover, even in this situation, where the link between politics and interpretive acts of a literary kind is close and pressuring, interpretive acts will still not be political acts in the strong sense, because while they might well have political consequences (by virtue of a network of reciprocal attention) they will still have as their immediate aim—as the purpose that gets them going—the telling of the truth about some text or group of texts. In the United States, literary interpretive acts are both limited in their immediate aim and without consequences outside the precincts in which that aim is properly taken, and therefore those who perform interpretive acts need not feel at their backs the pressure exerted by their civic and religious identities.

My correspondent's second point is more directly challenging. No matter where we live, he points out, we carry with us histories as members of racial or ethnic groups, social classes, and political parties that surely have an influence on the areas of scholarship to which we gravitate and the questions we think to ask when we do our academic work. This is certainly true, and I can offer my own experience as a corroborating, if imperfectly understood (by me), example. A second-generation American Jew and the first in my family to attend college, it can hardly be an accident that I have made my life's work non-dramatic literature of the sixteenth and seventeenth centuries, with a special emphasis on the relationship between Christian theology and aesthetic structures. Nor am I alone. I remember looking around my department at Berkeley in the late 1960s and saying (to myself), 'My God, all the Christian humanists are Jews.'

How is this phenomenon to be read? What does it mean? Presumably it means that for many young Jews of my generation the process of assimilation included a decision, less than consciously made, to identify with that part of the field most invested in the assumptions, both cultural and theological, of the mainstream tradition. But while such a consideration, however mediated, might well have been a reason (less than conscious) for my getting into a certain line of work, it was not a reason that guided me in *doing* that work once I became committed to it. That is, when I set out, for example, to account for the peculiarly astringent power of Herbert's poetry, I did not begin with an awareness of my position as a Jew explicating Christian verse; rather I began with an awareness of what had been done and said by those who had preceded me in attempting that task, and it was in reference to their prior efforts—with its record of successes, failures, and unresolved problems—that I mounted my own. What I am invoking here, despite my earlier jibes at the discipline of philosophy, is the familiar philosophical distinction between the context of justification—the context that determines what will count as evidence in the eyes and ears of one's peers—and the context of discovery—the personal history that brought one into this arena of evidence rather than into another.

This brings me to my correspondent's third point, which is, I think, the most telling: that in so far as the question is the relationship between academic practices and social or political change, it is finally 'a matter of degree, rather than of essence'. I couldn't agree more. In some countries—Israel would seem to be an example—academic and political practices, even in the case of literary studies, overlap to such an extent that one cannot engage in the former without having the latter strongly in mind (although, I would hasten to add, they remain distinctive, even when because of contingent circumstances, they become linked up). But in some other countries, and I have been saying that the United States is one, the overlap, while theoretically possible, is simply not a feature of the situation, and the two go their way with only chance meetings that will seem odd when they occur. This is not to deny that even in the United States alterations in the structure of academic life will sometimes have an effect on the society as a whole. As Catherine Gallagher has observed, new historicist and allied movements have already altered the institutional landscape by influencing 'curricula in literature departments . . . introducing non-canonical texts into the classroom . . .

making students . . . more aware of the history and significance of . . . imperialism, slavery and gender differentiation' (in H. Aram Veeser, ed., *The New Historicism*, New York, 1989, 44–5). And it is no doubt true that in some cases (although by no means all or even the majority) students introduced to these new texts and topics will factor them into their thinking in ways that will markedly affect their performances as citizens, churchgoers, parents, doctors, lawyers, etc. (The so-called 'Sixties' generation can stand as a convenient collective instance.) But, to repeat a point I have made often, such consequences of one's disciplinary activities cannot be counted on. They may or may not occur; and, more importantly, such consequences are not what one intends when engaging in a piece of literary analysis; not because such an intention is incapable of realization in any context, but because in the context now in force in the United States, it cannot be responsibly formed.

To this one might respond, 'So much the worse for the United States.' But I am not so sure. Being sequestered in the academy has its advantages as well as its liabilities; many who wished for increased public attention to their labours got it in the past few years of the right-wing backlash and found that, rather than bringing respect and influence, it brought danger and the elimination of progressive programmes. Perhaps it is not so bad a thing after all that in the United States those who operate the levers of commerce and government do not give much heed to what goes on in our classrooms or in our learned journals.

Again one must note the exception that proves the rule. In the years of the Reagan and Bush administrations a number of government officials had links to a network of Straussians, students and followers of the late Leo Strauss, a political philosopher who strongly attacked what he saw as the corrosive relativism of modern thought and urged a return to the normative thinking of the ancients. Strauss's views or versions of them were alive and well in the persons of William Bennett, Lynne Cheney, Chester Finn, Dianne Ravitch, and Quayle's Chief of Staff, William Kristol, and

it is at least arguable that these and others close to the adminis-
tration were able to influence its policies especially in matters of
education, the arts, and civil rights. It would seem, then, that this
was an instance in which intellectuals had a direct impact on the
political life of the nation. But if these men and women were
influential it was not because of their teachings and writings but
because they managed through non-academic connections to
secure positions that gave their teachings and writings a force
they would not have had if they had remained in the academy
where they would have had to wait for some accidental meeting
between their 'great thoughts' and the powers that be. Absent
such an accident or an appointment to public office only contin-
gently related to those thoughts (government officials don't say,
'He wrote a great book on the English novel; let's make him
Secretary of Education'), there are no regular routes by which the
accomplishments of academics in general and literary academics
in particular can be transformed into the currency of politics.

This is not an inevitable condition: there is nothing in theory
to prevent such routes from being established, but literary theorists will not be the people to establish them; the initiative has to
come from the other direction, from those who are so situated as
to have the power (although they do not yet have the reasons) to
introduce into their councils news from the world of cultural
studies, or feminist theory or reader-response criticism. As things
stand now such a development is not easily imaginable (and even
if it were realized, the news would have to be translated into
political terms, at which point it would no longer be literary), for
it would require alterations in the existing spheres of influence
and routes of communication so great that the culture of which
we are all members would be unrecognizable. Until that happens, or until some unlikely political event surprises us—such as,
for instance, the election to the presidency of a literary critic; and
in order for it to count he or she would have to be elected *as* a literary critic, and not as someone otherwise qualified who *also* laid
claim to this curious little talent—literary critics will have to be

content with the 'trickle-down' consequences that may or may
not flow from the fact that generations of young adults pass
through their classrooms. It goes without saying that such consequences—associated in earlier pedagogical fantasies with Mr
Chips—will not be sufficient for those who want to participate in
'the revolutionary transformation of social relations all at one go'
(Tony Bennett, *Outside Literature*, London, 1990, 237). All one can
offer such would-be shakers and movers is an unhappy choice:
they must either content themselves with the successes achieved
in the context of specifically literary goals and purposes, or they
must look forward to a life of continual frustration as the desire
to extend the effects of such successes into precincts incapable of
recognizing them (never mind responding to them) goes forever
unrealized.

The unhappiness of this choice has not been lost on those it
confronts. Critics who begin with 'revolutionary' aspirations
regularly lament the fact that their efforts have been appropriated—and, to add insult to injury, rewarded—by the very institution they thought to transcend. Immediately after claiming to
be reforming his own culture by reforming the received picture
of the culture of Spenser and Shakespeare, Montrose ruefully
acknowledges 'that my professional practice as a teacher-
scholar is also a vehicle for my partly unconscious and partly
calculating negotiation of disciplinary, institutional, and societal
demands and expectations' ('Professing the Renaissance', in
Veeser, ed., *The New Historicism*, 30). 'I have', he admits, 'a complex and substantial stake in sustaining and reproducing the
very institutions whose operations I wish to call into question.'
In the same vein, Don Wayne worries that in the work of new
historicists power relations replace other themes in what
amounts to little more than a 'new formalism'. The danger, he
observes, is that the new terms, with their apparent political
edge, will 'operate in our criticism in the way that generic categories, narrative functions, and stylistic devices did formerly'
('Power, Politics, and the Shakespearean Text', in J. Howard and

M. O'Connor, eds., *Shakespeare Reproduced: The Text in History and Ideology*, New York, 1987, 61). That is, they will operate as components of a practice that continues to be shaped by the imperative to explicate poems. The face of the practice may continually change as new topics are drawn into its orbit, but, once in, anything 'new' is immediately rendered very familiar by the questions—with what does it cohere? of what is it a conversion? with what is it in tension?—the practice is obliged (by its own sense of itself) to ask. That is why supposedly 'critical scholarship', scholarship driven by the determination to read 'against the grain', is, as Michael Bristol sadly notes, 'likely to result in legitimation rather than in practically effective critique' ('Lenten Butchery: Legitimation Crisis in *Coriolanus*', in Howard and O'Connor, eds., *Shakespeare Reproduced*, 220), likely, in other words to extend rather than challenge the discipline that finds room for it. 'Just at the moment when its presence in the . . . university seems assured,' John Beverley laments, 'cultural studies has begun to lose the radicalizing force that accompanied its emergence as a field' (*Against Literature*, Minneapolis, 1993, 21).

The fear that this loss has already been suffered haunts a huge anthology entitled *Cultural Studies* (ed. Lawrence Grossberg, Cary Nelson, and Paula Treichler, New York, 1992), the record of a conference held at the University of Illinois in 1990. The papers at that conference were many and varied in their focus, but they shared a desire to link the practice of cultural studies in the classroom to the project of restructuring society. In almost every question period, however, someone would raise the obvious point that this very meeting, with all of its talk about interventions, radical questionings, and transgressions, was taking place at a large, publicly funded university and bore all the marks of the hierarchies, factional rivalries, and personal agendas that were so often the objects of scathing criticism. Where at a different kind of conference a speaker might have been challenged because he cited an outdated edition or failed to take account of newly discovered facts, a speaker at this conference was challenged because 'a certain Eurocentrism' (368) had been detected in his argument. He replied in kind, finding the comments of his questioner 'problematic' because 'you seek to give them moral force by situating yourself as a representative of a number of marginalized or repressed constituencies' (368). The game here is not 'my scholarship is better than yours', but 'my marginalization is greater and more authentic than yours', but the difference is, as Chomsky might say, a notational variant, and at bottom the games are pretty much the same.

This sense of the game weighs heavily on the participants who wish they were not playing it, but doing something else. 'I don't mind listening to people I admire,' one participant declares, 'but it seems to me we need four days of discussion about how we can intervene in the institutions in which we work, rather than four days reproducing the same kind of hierarchy we already have' (294). It is hard to see why he thinks that an additional four days would be less shadowed by the institutions that would structure and sponsor them or less hierarchical in their unfolding than the days he has already endured, or more likely to produce strategies other than those he has learned to perform in the schools he now despises. 'What we have to understand', says another participant, 'is that we too are held by institutionalized practices and discourses . . . I'm often frustrated with my own inability to rethink these standard practices' (528–9). Stuart Hall is more than frustrated; he is 'completely dumbfounded' by American cultural studies, which seems to him the very emblem of the 'moment of profound danger' that always attends 'institutionalization' (285). If that is the danger, it surrounds this conference; it *is* this conference.

The basic point has been made with devastating authority by Evan Watkins. Academic literary work, he says,

occupies a marginal position and circulation within the dominant formation. And studying TV commercials or films or rock music or political speeches rather than a 'traditional' literary canon does little in and of itself to effect any social change. That sort of 'territory shift' doesn't

[100]

mean we're now playing for big stakes . . . It just means we're playing for the same marginal stakes with new material . . . that the one-way street remains a dead end, unable to convey the work involved anywhere else. (*Work Time: English Departments and the Circulation of Cultural Value*, Stanford, Calif., 1989, 271.)

After such things have been said, it is hard to imagine saying anything else. But the dream of intervening in the world more effectively than the profession of literary criticism seems to allow dies hard. Within a few paragraphs Watkins is urging his readers/ colleagues to 'forge connections to popular cultures . . . and to use the connections to educate a support structure for the next step, the next shift in territory in a prolonged war of position' (273), and in the penultimate sentence of his book he is calling on his fellow critics 'to change the conditions of all our work' (276). It could be that in time all or almost all of the conditions of our work might be changed (as they have in fact changed since the days of Sidney, Jonson, and Milton), but the change will not come about because literary critics have *willed* it; for we could change the conditions of all our work only by standing outside them (but then it is hard to say why they would then be *our* conditions). So long as we labour within them the changes we might make will be in the nature of modifications rather than ruptures. If, for example, we 'forge connections to popular culture' by writing about it in addition to or in place of writing about Shakespeare and Spenser we will merely have added another room to our academic house. This will make a difference in the way the profession looks, but it will not mean that the boundaries of the profession will have been pushed outward. Bringing new grist to your mill does not in itself alter the basic manner of its operation. It would seem from much of his book that Watkins knows this, but the knowledge weighs heavily on him and when the lure of political hope captures him, he forgets it.

Sometimes the forgetting is instantaneous. Montrose asserts strongly (and correctly) that the 'possibility of political and institutional agency cannot be based upon the illusion of an escape

WHY LITERARY CRITICISM IS LIKE VIRTUE

from ideology' ('Professing the Renaissance', 30), of an escape, that is, from the presuppositions within which one thinks to act. However, the very next sentence begins with 'However': 'However, the very process of subjectively *living* the confrontations or contradictions within or among ideologies makes it possible to experience facets of our own subjection . . . to read, as in a refracted light, one fragment of our ideological inscription by means of another.' Montrose underlines 'living', but what he really means by it is 'thinking about' or 'being self-consciously aware of'. The idea is that while ideological subjection is unavoidable, we can at least gain a perspective on it, either by moving back and forth 'among' ideological formations in a way that gives us a purchase on one even as we are 'inscribed' in another, or by surfacing the contradictions 'within' an ideology and thus distancing ourselves from its full sway. We may not be able to escape ideology, but we can, in moments of strenuous self-consciousness, loosen its hold.

There are two theses here. The first is that every ideological formation gains its apparent plausibility only by suppressing elements within it that would, if they were brought to light, subvert its claims to coherence. The second thesis is that once we are aware of this truth about a particular ideology, its force will have been lessened, if only slightly. ('A reflexive knowledge so partial and unstable may, nevertheless, provide subjects with a means of empowerment as agents.') The first thesis seems to me obviously right: when the apparent unity of an ideological system is strongly interrogated one will always discover the embarrassing exceptions, concessions, and barely disguised duplicities that tell the 'real story' of an agenda cobbled together out of the most disparate and contradictory elements. An easy, because familiar to me, example is the body of American contract law, which ceaselessly presents a master narrative in which autonomous agents freely enter into bargained-for-exchanges that courts inspect only for procedural flaws while refusing on principle to import into their rulings any considerations of value. But even a cursory knowledge of the case-law reveals that this master narrative is kept afloat by invoking (under rubrics like unconscionability) just those considerations that have been most loudly banished by the rhetoric of the enterprise. In its every operation contract law is telling *two* stories while pretending that the second one has been ruled out of court.

Should we conclude then (as proponents of the Critical Legal Studies movement tend to) that this news should be broadcast from the rooftops, and that if it were, a shamefaced profession would give up its shabby ways and face the basic contradictions of its inauthentic existence? I'm afraid not, if only because this is news that everyone already knows, and not only knows but uti-lizes in the course of getting through the mercantile and juridical day. It is by virtue of the contradictions it harbours that contract law is able to exhibit the flexibility required by the double obli-gation to adhere to an official morality of contractual autonomy while adjusting its rulings to the reality of a world in which such autonomy has always and already been compromised. An analy-sis of contract law that foregrounded its contradictions would be embarrassing to its project only if the goal of that project were to be philosophically consistent. But that is not the goal of any pro-ject except for the project of philosophy itself. Other projects have the less abstract goal (which philosophy also shares) of wanting to flourish. I would have thought that the last word on the relationship between the foregrounding of contradiction and the impulse to reform was said by Joe E. Brown in Billy Wilder's classic movie *Some Like It Hot*. Brown, you will remember, has been courting Jack Lemmon in drag and is about to propose to him on a boat. Thinking to end this farce once and for all by revealing a fatal contradiction in the structure of Brown's desire, Lemmon cries, 'I can't marry you; I'm a man', to which Brown sublimely replies, 'Nobody's perfect.'

The moral here is that the awareness of contradiction doesn't make any necessary difference and certainly will not make the difference (claimed by Montrose) of allowing us at once to experience constraint (or as he calls it subjection) and to stand apart from it. This is the hope and the dream of critical self-consciousness, the thesis that ye shall know that what passes for the truth is socially and historically constructed and that knowledge shall set you free. The critically self-conscious agent, the argument goes, is just as embedded as anyone else, but he is *aware* of it and that makes all the difference, or at least the difference that keeps the hope of boundary-breaking behaviour alive. This will work, however, only if the knowledge that we are embedded is stored in a part of the mind that floats free of the embeddedness we experience at any one time; but that would mean that at least a part of our mind was not somewhere but everywhere and that would mean that we were not human beings but gods. In a frankly religious tradition the internalization of deity is not only possible, it is obligatory; but in the militantly secular tradition of the new historicism and cultural studies, what is internalized are the routines and deep assumptions of human practices which resemble deity only in that they are jealous of rivals and say to us 'Thou shalt have no other gods before me'.

Critical self-consciousness, conceived of as a mental action independent of the setting in which it occurs, is the last infirmity of the mind that would deny its own limits by positioning itself in two places at the same time, in the place of its local embodiment and in the disembodied place (really no place) of reflection. It is to this latter place that cultural studies promises to bring us by relaxing the grip of forms of thought and categorization specific to particular disciplines. It should be the 'result of practicing Cultural Studies', declares Fred Inglis, 'that they teach both the feasibility *and* the moral necessity of . . . displacement of the self into the fourth dimension' (*Cultural Studies*, Oxford, 1993, 210). By the 'fourth dimension', Inglis means a dimension removed from the pressures of everyday institutional and political life: 'I detach myself from myself and consider my life as if it were not mine, considering by what historical road it came to this pass.'

Refreshed by this sojourn in the ether of disembodied reflection, Inglis reports, 'I step back into myself, and the torrential demands of my life.'

In an older tradition this is the sequence enacted by penitents, pilgrims, and flagellants who ascend not to Cultural Studies but to the mount of Contemplation (see *The Faerie Queene*, I. x) and a vision of deity (see Plato's *Phaedrus* and Augustine's *On Christian Doctrine*). Cultural studies, it would seem, has replaced poetry as the replacement for religion; it is the new altar before which those who would cast off their infirmities worship. Cultural studies, Inglis intones only half-jokingly, 'will make you good' (229). Henry Giroux isn't joking at all when he declares that 'cultural studies offers the possibility for extending the democratic principles of justice, liberty, and equality to the widest possible set of social relations and institutional practices that constitute everyday life' (*Cultural Studies Times*, Fall 1994, A15). Somewhat less dramatically, but no less ambitiously, S. P. Mohanty finds in cultural and political criticism the key to being fully human 'not merely the capacity to act purposefully but also to *evaluate* actions and purposes in terms of larger ideas we might hold about, say, our political and moral world' ('Us and Them: On the Philosophical Bases of Political Criticism', *Yale Journal of Criticism*, 2/2, 1989, 22). It is this 'capacity for self-aware historical agency' that informs cultural–political criticism and is presumably enlarged by it. A discipline that resists this 'second order understanding' refuses to know the conditions of its own possibility and, in Bruce Robbins's words, 'shirks the responsibility to think through the issue of its own vocation, its own authorities, its own grounding' (*Secular Vocations*, London, 1993, 110).

These claims for the effects of cultural studies follow from (and are the mirror image of) the description of cultural studies as a more inclusive, deeper form of inquiry than is permitted by the self-policing parameters of traditional disciplines. My response to that description is also my response to this expression of hoped-for effects: cultural studies is not larger or more penetrating than the modes of interrogation it seeks to displace; it is merely different and will bring different—not higher or truer—yields. And while it will bring you to a different place than, say, the study of Renaissance pastoral, it will not bring you to any fourth dimension, only to the dimension of its own *specialized* practice. The practice of cultural studies will not make you good, it will make you proficient in the routines that are its content. Cultural studies involves no 'second-order' understanding, only the understanding of the phenomena its questions bring into view.

Moreover, what is true of cultural studies is true of reflection in general, that mode of mental activity of which cultural studies is supposedly the institutional form. It is not that reflection is impossible—most of us engage in it every day; it is just that rather than floating above the practices that are its object and providing a vantage-point from which those practices can be assessed and reformed, reflection is either (*a*) an activity *within* a practice and therefore finally not distanced from that practice's normative assumptions or (*b*) an activity grounded in its own normative assumptions and therefore one whose operations will reveal more about itself than about any practice viewed through its lens. If, for example, I 'reflect' on the relationship between literary studies and the study of history, the course of my reflection—the direction it takes—will be a function of the fact that literary studies (and everything it presupposes) is its starting-point. Such a reflection will yield answers, but they will be answers to the questions literary studies (as it is now constituted) poses and not to its own questions, and if they *were* the answers to reflection's own questions—to questions posed in reflection's own language, a language in no way hostage to literary imperatives—the answers could not be connected up with literary studies (or anything else) in anything but an arbitrary way. While it is always possible to interrogate a literary work by applying to it the categories of some philosophical system, absent any pre-established link between that system and the work's origin in an intentional project, the resulting description will be without any particular significance or, rather, will be available to any significance an interpreter happens to prefer. Again, either reflection is the extension of a practice and can claim no distance from it or it is itself a practice and has no privileged relationship to, or even any necessary significance for, practices other than itself.

What this means, as I argue elsewhere (in *Doing what Comes Naturally*, Oxford, 1989, ch. 19), is that there is no such thing as critical self-consciousness, no separate 'muscle of the mind' that can be flexed in any situation, no capacity either innate or socially nurtured for abstracting oneself from everyday routines in the very act of performing them, no buffer zone that allows us to assess critically what we are doing, no possibility of a discipline's thinking through 'the issue of its own grounding', no strategy for loosening the constraints that bind us whenever we set ourselves a particular task. And what *that* means is that any rewards or pleasures we might look for will come from particular tasks and not from their transcendence.

What are those rewards and pleasures? This is again the question of justification, now given new urgency because, in light of the arguments I have been making, the usual justifications are unpersuasive. The old justification made literary critics the custodians of a human treasure, a repository of wisdom good for all problems and all times. The new justification, fashioned by deconstructionists, new historicists, cultural materialists, postmodernists, etc., gives literary critics, now called discourse analysts, a role in the forming of new subjectivities capable of forming a counter-disciplinary practice as part of the construction of an 'oppositional public sphere' (Patrick Brantlinger, *Crusoe's Footprints*, New York, 1990, 24). The old justification won't work because the strong historicism to which many of us have been persuaded rules out a set of texts that float above all historical conditions dispensing wisdom to those fit to receive it. The new justification won't work because the same strong historicism leaves no room for the special and ahistorical brand of reflective consciousness that discourse analysis supposedly engenders.

If literary interpretation will neither preserve the old order nor create a new one, what can it do and why should anyone practise it? I can't tell you in so many words—a general answer to the question is precisely what my argument will not allow—but perhaps I can show you. My vehicle will be a single line from *Paradise Lost*. It occurs mid-way in book I, just as Milton's narrator is about to call the roll of fallen angels, who, he says, will in future times pass themselves off as gods to credulous mortals. They manage to so corrupt 'the greatest part of Mankind' (367–8) that men and women 'forsake God | their creator' (379) and fall to worshipping brutes. The contempt the narrator feels for those who are thus deceived is bitingly expressed in the line that interests me:

And Devils to adore for Deities. (373)

That is, how stupid can you be? Of all the mistakes to make, the mistaking of a devil for a deity seems the most reprehensible and the most inexplicable. How could you fail to tell the difference between the creator and the most base of his creatures, hardly a creature at all in his rebellious infidelity? That is surely the sense of the line, at least in paraphrase which, if it is a heresy, is one we all necessarily and endlessly practise.

But, even as that sense unfolds, the medium of its expression begins to undo it; for while the sense of the line insists on the great difference between devils and deities and registers incredulity at anyone's inability to tell them apart, the sound-pattern of the line—what would have been called in Milton's age its 'schematic figures'—is blurring the difference and making it hard to tell them apart. Not only are the two main nouns, Devils and Deities, linked by alliteration and assonance, but their acoustic similarity is quite literally mirrored in the words—'to adore for'—that separate them, but do not really separate them since the effect of mirroring is to bring them even closer together.

[108]

What then is the line finally saying: that there is a huge difference between devils and deities or that there is practically (a word precisely intended) no difference between devils and deities? The answer—inevitable given the underlying assumptions of literary interpretation as I described them earlier—is that the line is saying both: the difference is huge; the difference is very small, and there is no paradox because the largeness and smallness exist on different levels. The difference is small if we think to discern it with the physical eye or ear. Devils can make themselves up to look or sound like deities any time; appearance, after all, is the diabolical realm, is what they worship, is what they are. True discernment requires an *inner* eye capable of penetrating to essences, an eye that does not rest on surfaces, but quite literally sees through them, the eye in short, of faith, famously defined in Hebrews 11 as the 'evidence of things not seen'. The inner eye has only God as its object; and the difference between God and anything else looms large and immediately; if the gaze wanders, if the eye is distracted by some glittering simulacrum, the difference is blurred and becomes difficult to 'tell'. Those who mistake devils for deities do not experience an empirical failure; they experience the failure that is empiricism, the failure to distinguish between the things that are made and the maker, who is, of course, invisible.

The failure that is empiricism is graphically on display in book II when Mammon, admiring the 'Gems and Gold' beneath the soil of hell, declares 'what can Heav'n show more?' (273). He really means it; for Mammon there is nothing more than show, appearance, surface; that is all he can see—and hell to adore for heaven—because that is all he is. The master text for all of this is the *Areopagitica*:

Good and evill . . . in the field of the World grow up together almost inseparably; and the knowledge of good is so involv'd and interwoven with the knowledge of evill, and in so many cunning resemblances hardly to be discern'd, that those confused seeds which were imposed

[109]

on *Psyche* as an incessant labour to cull out, and sort asunder, were not more intermixed. (*Complete Prose Works*, ii. 514)

Both the difficulty and the necessity of discerning are Milton's great subject and he presents it by repeatedly displaying 'cunning resemblances' and then asking his readers to sort them asunder. The result is 'incessant labour', an interpretive labour, whose yield is not the calculation of the right answer but the experience of how difficult it is 'in the field of this World' to determine what the right answer is, how difficult it is to tell the difference between devils and deities.

For me the reward and pleasure of literary interpretation lie in being able to perform analyses like this. Literary interpretation, like virtue, is its own reward. I do it because I like the way I feel when I'm doing it. I like being brought up short by an effect I have experienced but do not yet understand analytically. I like trying to describe in flatly prosaic words the achievement of words that are anything but flat and prosaic. I like savouring the physical 'taste' of language at the same time that I work to lay bare its physics. I like uncovering the incredibly dense pyrotechnics of a master artificer, not least because in praising the artifice I can claim a share in it. And when those pleasures have been (temporarily) exhausted, I like linking one moment in a poem to others and then to moments in other works, works by the same author or by his predecessors or contemporaries or successors. It doesn't finally matter which, so long as I can *keep going*, reaping the cognitive and tactile harvest of an activity as self-reflexive as I become when I engage in it.

It is no small irony that in making this confession I have come round to the very position Terry Eagleton articulates when he declares 'what the aesthetic imitates in its very glorious futility, in its pointless self-referentiality, in all its full-blooded formalism, is nothing less than human existence itself, which needs no rationale beyond its own self-delight, which is an end in itself and which will stoop to no external determination' ('The Ideology of the Aesthetic', in S. Regan, ed., *The Politics of Pleasure: Aesthetics and Cultural Theory*, Buckingham, Penn., 1992, 30). I couldn't have said it better, and I also agree with that part of Eagleton's analysis which finds aesthetic pleasure operating both as a support and guarantor of dominant modes of thought and as a challenge to those same modes. But at the moment I am neither supporting nor challenging, but just plain enjoying.

Indeed I will take my enjoyment wherever I can find it. Thus when I run out of sources and analogues, similarities and differences, I go to the history of the criticism which not only allows me to continue the game, but to secure my place in it by linking my own efforts to those of past giants. In the case of 'And Devils to adore for Deities' I would head straight back to F. R. Leavis and his famously infamous attack on Milton's style, which, he says, 'compels an attitude toward itself that is incompatible with sharp concrete realization' ('Milton's Verse', in C. A. Patrides, ed., *Milton's Epic Poetry*, Baltimore, 1967, 22). That is, rather than pointing the reader to something beyond itself, Milton's language, Leavis complains, calls attention to itself, to the relationships between its components. Milton 'exhibits a feeling *for* words rather than a capacity for feeling *through* words'. For Leavis, this refusal of the lived complexities of sensuous experience in favour of a verbal universe that traps us in its own intricacies is a fault of both style and character. The character is 'disastrously single-minded' (28) and its narcissistic obsessiveness is reflected in a 'tyrannical stylization' that in its 'remoteness' (22) from English speech totally ignores the needs of the reader. Milton, Leavis concludes, 'often produces passages that have to be read through several times before one can see how they go' (24).

To all of this I would say 'precisely so', but where Leavis sees perversity and a 'defect of imagination' (28), I see an intention brilliantly realized. The intention is to make the verse of the poem into a set of exercises in which the reader is forced to confront the difficulty of interpretive choices that must nevertheless be made. In relation to this intention the last thing Milton wants us to do is feel through his words to something else; rather he wants to *arrest* our attention, to slow down the reading experience to the extent that *its* problems become its content. It is just as Leavis says: the words of the poem *do* 'value themselves . . . highly' (26), occupying our attention to the exclusion of any referent beyond them; but that is because the field of reference Milton is interested in is abstract, is a philological and philosophical field populated by the great moral and theological problems with which the age was obsessed. It is, to borrow a phrase from Francis Bacon, 'a country in the mind', and if Milton wants us to remain in it and undergo its salutary trials, he must prevent us from escaping into the rich particulars of Leavis's 'concretely realized' world. If 'passages have to be read through several times before one can see how they go', it is because the *cognitive* acts such readings and rereadings involve are the acts Milton wants us to perform.

I see that in the course of presenting an example of literary criticism I have fallen under the sway of its imperatives and am now pursuing my analysis seriously rather than as a mere illustration. That's the way it is for me. I can't stay away from the stuff. It's what I do; and that, finally, is the only justification I can offer for its practice. It is usually said that justification, in order to be valid, must not borrow its terms from the activity being justified. Only a justification that did not presuppose the value of the activity under scrutiny would be legitimate; otherwise one would be trading on a value while pretending to establish it. This picture of justification will work, however, only if there is a normative structure in relation to which any and all practices can be assessed; but if, as I have been arguing, there is no such structure and each practice is answerable to the norms implicit in its own history and conventions, then justification can only proceed *within* that history and in relation to those conventions. It is not that an external justification could not be mounted, but that it would tell you more about the justificatory mechanism than about the enterprise supposedly being justified. Justification is always internal and can only get off the ground if the value it seeks to uncover or defend is presupposed and is (surreptitiously) guiding the process at the end of which it is triumphantly revealed. Justification never starts from scratch, and can only begin if everything it seeks to demonstrate is already taken for granted.

It is because justification is internal and never starts from scratch that no one chooses a profession by surveying available options and settling on the one whose claims to moral and philosophical coherence seem most persuasive. (The scenario is the same one that imagines Montrose *choosing* to believe in his readings of Spenser and Shakespeare.) Choice of that kind is never the route by which you 'discover' your life's work; rather, one day, after many false starts, or in the wake of 'starts' you do not recall attempting, you find yourself in the middle of doing something, enmeshed in its routines, extending in every action its assumptions. And when the request for justification comes, you respond *from the middle*, respond with the phrases and platitudes of disciplinary self-congratulation, respond with a rehearsal of canonical achievements and ancient claims to universal benefit, respond, as Weinrib says, by ploughing over the same ground in ever deeper furrows. Justification is not a chain of inferences, but a circle, and it proceeds, if that is the word, by telling a story in which every detail is an instantiation of an informing spirit that is known only in the details but always exceeds them.

Moreover, it is hard, if not impossible, to tell that story to those who do not already know it, or, rather, are not already living it. If you ask me, 'Why is it a good thing to explicate *Paradise Lost?*', I can do nothing better or more persuasive than *do* it, spinning it out in directions at once familiar and surprising, ringing the changes, sounding the notes in the hope that the song is one you know or that it will be infectious enough to start you singing. Literary interpretation, Michael Carter has recently said, has no purpose external to the arena of its practice; it is the 'constant unfolding' to ourselves 'of who we are' as practitioners; its audience is made up of those who already thrill to its challenges and resonate to its performances (Michael Carter, 'Scholarship as Rhetoric of Display', *College English*, 54/3, Mar. 1992, 310). Richard Rorty makes the same point when he rejects the idea that 'humanities departments should have aims'—goals external to their own obsessions—and counsels us simply to think of departments as oases for 'a bunch of wayfaring pilgrims who happened to take shelter in the same inn, or in the same section of the stacks' ('Tales of Two Disciplines', *Callalou*, 17/2, 1994, 575). That's all there is to it; there's nothing more to be said, but it's enough for those who long ago ceased to be able to imagine themselves living any other life. Last year, an old friend whom I hadn't seen for a while called me to catch up. 'What are you doing this summer?' he asked. 'Writing on *Paradise Lost*,' I answered. 'But that's what you said thirty years ago,' he responded. 'Right,' I replied, 'yet once more'; and if I had thought of it I would have borrowed a line from my friend David Lodge, who borrowed it from George and Ira Gershwin: 'Nice work if you can get it'.

Public Justification and Public
Intellectuals

BUT can you get it? The question acknowledges what everybody knows, that the academic literary enterprise is under siege, and that in an age of shrinking budgets and demands for accountability, a justificatory rhetoric that remains internal to the profession may be, to say the least, counter-productive. I have just insisted that we should respond to the demand for justification not by looking to some value or goal external to a discipline's history and traditions, but by rehearsing in ever greater detail and with much enthusiasm that history and by extending, in exemplary pieces of practice, those traditions; literary studies are not valuable because of what they might lead to—the recovery of a moral compass or the emergence of a truly emancipated subject—but because of what they already are, where the content of 'already are' is the array of challenges and tasks left to us by our predecessors, and the pleasures of rising to the challenges and completing (for a time, at least) the tasks. I stand by this account of justification (which is in fact a refusal of its demand), but I realize that as an internal account it conceives only of an internal audience, an audience made up of fellow prac-titioners, and, perhaps, of the parents of practitioners who are forever wondering why and how it is that their offspring have hit upon such a curious way to make (or not make) a living. What do we say to those not of our party without whose approval and material/political support that living could not be made? What do we say to the *public*, that generalized body that wants, not unreasonably, to believe that the cultural activities it sustains have a benign relationship to its concerns and values?

It is at this point in any discussion that the topic of the 'public intellectual' will be raised, and will be quickly followed by a diatribe against specialization—against the unwillingness of academic practitioners to look beyond the confines and imperatives of their disciplines—and a call for the return of intellectuals who speak not only to their peers about merely professional matters, but to 'broader audiences on broader issues' (Janny Scott, 'Journeys from Ivory Tower: Public Intellectual is Reborn', *New York Times*, 8 Aug. 1994, A1). It is not clear whether we are *all* being urged to become public intellectuals (which would certainly overcrowd the field even before it got established) or whether only some of us should take up this task while the rest of us continue to labour in the ever smaller vineyards of the academy. Assuming that it is the second course of action that is being urged, one wonders what the public intellectual will be able to say to his 'broader audience' that will make the members of that audience happy to sustain those intellectuals whose audience remains each other? Or will he ally himself with the public he serves and denounce his less media-savvy former colleagues? (That is, in fact, what tends to happen.)

As interesting as these questions are, however, they must wait upon the posing of a prior question: how does one get to be a public intellectual (as opposed to an intellectual studying Latin metrics or medieval armaments) in the first place? If you read the *New York Times* and other popular media organs, you would think it a matter of simple choice, and some academics seem themselves to be of this opinion. 'I am increasingly dissatisfied', says one, 'with speaking to a few people and want to speak to more' ('Journeys from Ivory Tower', B4). Well, that's nice, but I'm afraid it's not that easy. Almost everyone wants to speak to more people, but the trick is getting those people to listen or even to hear you. If you want to speak to Miltonists or to historians of early modern Europe, you know what to do: take a degree in an accredited institution, secure a position in a department, write for the appropriate journals, and attach yourself to the various networks that link people who have gravitated toward the 'same section of the stacks'. But if you want to speak to the public, there is no degree to be had, no accepted course of accreditation, no departments of Public Relevance (there are of course departments of Public Policy, but they won't get you an audience beyond that made up of the members of other departments of Public Policy), and above all, no network of conferences, journals, fellowships, and chaired professorships that give the enterprise a material stability. What this means is that were you to wake up one morning and say to yourself, 'I think I'll become a public intellectual,' there would be no roadway or sequence of steps whose negotiation would lead to the implementation of your new resolve.

It would seem then that the prior question, 'How does one get to be a public intellectual?', must itself wait upon the posing of an even more prior question: 'What is a public intellectual anyway?' As it is used in recent polemics, the term gets its force from the binary opposite implied by it: the private intellectual. But there are no private intellectuals, or at least none that count in this discussion (there *are* 'independent scholars'), for as Andrew Ross observes, the academy 'is a massive public sphere in itself, involving millions of people in this country alone, and so the idea that you break out of the academy into the public is rather a nonsense' (*Cultural Studies Times*, 1/2, Fall 1994, A11).

One can reply to this, as Bruce Robbins does, by distinguishing between the obviously public space taken up by academics and the disinclination of so many of them to reach out to the inhabitants of other public spaces, a disinclination that amounts to a self-imposed 'marginality' (*Secular Vocations*, 97). It is this marginality, says Robbins, that 'has to some extent been fought off' by 'politically charged interdisciplinary projects like cultural studies, whose collapsing of the elite/popular divide and democratizing of subject matter give it another claim to public responsiveness'

(97). But Robbins here forgets the Foucauldian lesson he elsewhere teaches: marginality *is* a public role, and one that had considerable power when it was widely assumed in the culture that the nourishing of the private imagination was a necessary preparation for the performance of public service. Because that assumption is no longer in place, marginality is no longer an attractive—that is, effective—public pose. But it is more than a pose: it is a fact inseparable from the myriad facts of academic institutional life as they have been described in these pages; and, as I have argued repeatedly, these are not facts that can be dispelled by the installation, in this same academic institution, of 'politically charged interdisciplinary projects like cultural studies'. A public intellectual is not someone who takes as his or her subject matters of public concern—every law professor does that; a public intellectual is someone who takes as his or her subject matters of public concern, and *has the public's attention*. Since one cannot gain that attention from the stage of the academy (except by some happy contingency), academics, by definition, are not candidates for the role of public intellectual. Whatever the answer to the question 'How does one get to be a public intellectual?', we know that it *won't* be 'by joining the academy'.

That doesn't mean that academics do not appear in public. In the past few days alone, I have seen peering out from my television screen a number of friends, acquaintances, and fellow professors: David Brion Davis, Arthur Schlesinger, Nadine Strossen, Catherine MacKinnon, Camille Paglia. And on other days I have found myself watching and listening to Henry Louis Gates, Christina Hoff Sommers, Noam Chomsky, Randall Kennedy, Alan Derschowitz, Stephen Carter, Stephen Balch, Edward Said, Leonard Jeffries, Catharine Stimpson, Walter Dellinger, Lawrence Tribe, Shelby Steele, Harold Bloom, Carl Sagan. The list could easily be doubled and even quadrupled, and everyone on it would be an academic, but no one of them would be a public intellectual; rather they would be 'rent for a day' intellectuals or 'cameo' intellectuals—persons brought in either because they

are considered authorities on a particular issue (the media equivalent of an expert witness) or because they hold a position on that
same issue that can be theatrically opposed to the position of
another well-credentialled professor. (This is the *Nightline* view of
the world, a universe populated by people wearing glasses and
saying differently extreme things about every subject under the
sun.) Thus, if Nadine Strossen is there you know that some First
Amendment question (woman in Muslim dress detained because
she is suspected of hiding her identity) is in the news; and if
Catherine MacKinnon is there you know she is being counted on
to disagree with Strossen. If Christina Hoff Sommers is there
you know that the subject is feminism and that the producers
wanted to be able to display a certified anti-feminist feminist; and
if the occasion is a panel discussion, Sommers might be joined by
Camille Paglia (although the small screen is probably not big
enough for both of them) and Catharine Stimpson might be
placed in the middle, both literally and figuratively. If racism
rather than feminism is the subject, the assembled panel might
include Jeffries, Gates, Steele, and either Kennedy or Carter (one
lawyer is always enough); and if the topic is political correctness
(oh no, not again), Stimpson might disengage herself from the
feminist dialogue and do verbal battle with Stephen Balch.

These and the others on my list will only get the call when the
particular issue with which they are identified takes centre-stage
and should that issue lose its sexiness, their media careers will be
over. That is why they are 'cameo' intellectuals or intellectuals
for a day; a public intellectual, on the other hand, is the *public's*
intellectual; that is, he or she is someone to whom the public regularly looks for illumination on any number of (indeed all) issues
and, as things stand now, the public does not look to academics
for this *general* wisdom, in part because (as is often complained)
academics are not trained to speak on everything, only on particular things, but more importantly because academics do not have
a stage or a pulpit from which their pronouncements, should
they be inclined to make them, could be broadcast.

I say 'as things stand now' because academics, or least a visible number of them, once did have such a pulpit, the college presidency or major deanship, offices that for a long time carried with them not only the possibility but the obligation of addressing issues of public concern. The same *New York Times* that in August of 1994 added its voice to those calling for the return of the public intellectual reported in September of 1994 on a pattern that did much to explain why that call will find no response beyond its own (rhetorical) echo:

A generation ago, James B. Conant of Harvard, Clark Kerr of the University of California, Robert M. Hutchins of the University of Chicago and a great many other college and university presidents cut striking figures on the public stage.

They called for the reform of American education, proposed safeguards for democracy, sought to defuse the Cold War, urged moral standards for scientific research and addressed other important issues of the time.

Today almost no college or university president has spoken out significantly about Bosnia, Haiti, North Korea, welfare reform, the attack on the National Endowment for the Arts or dozens of other issues high on the national agenda. (Reprinted in the *Raleigh News and Observer*, 4 Sept. 1994, 17A)

There is no dearth of explanations for this change—the pressures of fund-raising and a reluctance to offend potential donors, the increased complexity and volume of administrative work, the emergence of a new (and convenient for the timid) conviction that 'a high university official could not take a position on a social issue without inhibiting the freedom of dissent'—but whatever the explanation, the result is a campus culture in which the people at the top have repudiated the very behaviour that public intellectuals are supposed to engage in. I am not saying that if university presidents were to reclaim the forum they have relinquished, rank-and-file faculty would follow their example, but I am saying that the *negative* example of college presidents is one more indication of how much the demand that academics be public intellectuals is at odds with the conditions, conceptual and institutional, in relation to which their labours are intelligible and marketable.

Nevertheless, that demand continues to be made, not only from the outside, but on the inside, where it is one more manifestation of the unhappy desire of the humanist scholar to be more than he is. A recent example is provided by Michael Bérubé in his book *Public Access: Literary Theory and American Cultural Politics* (London, 1994). Bérubé traverses much of the territory I have negotiated in these lectures, and at times his insights seem to coincide with mine, as when he warns against 'a critical slippage between two meanings of "politics," broad and narrow' because it 'leads the cultural left to think it's more subversive than it is, and it leads the cultural right to affect outrage that literary and cultural critics are engaged in "politics" as if we were interfering with trade agreements or filibustering a jobs bill' (35). I nod even more vigorously when, echoing Stuart Hall, he declares 'it's one thing to realize that intellectual work is political . . . it's another thing to think you've conquered hegemony just by talking about it' (154).

But these moments of rueful modesty are few and far between; more typical is some expression of the hope that the academic cultural left will be able first to win over, and then to transform, the larger society that now misunderstands and mistrusts it. It is time, Bérubé says, to stop underestimating our 'potential for winning the informed support of meaningful numbers of non-academics', time to 'win new constituencies among aspiring educators and professionals, new constituencies on the progressive-but-not-poststructuralist left, and . . . new constituencies in what we must help to make a broader and more diverse public sphere' (81, 112). Ringing words, but they provoke a simple question: 'how?' By what vehicle are we to do these things?

The answer turns out to be (you guessed it) 'cultural studies', for when 'cultural studies engages with the popular and the "ordinary" it does so primarily in order to understand—and thereby try to *change*—the power relations that shape the most intimate and/or quotidian details of our lives' (140). There are two assertions here, and there is more of a relationship between them in Bérubé's sentence than there is in the real world. The first assertion, undoubtedly true, is that cultural studies takes as the object of its attention the power relations that structure our lives; but the second assertion is that by doing so cultural studies works to change those relations, which only provokes in an even more insistent form the question 'how?' How does the work of cultural studies, conducted in the professional spaces of the academy, do the work of changing the culture it studies?

Bérubé has an answer: cultural studies will do culture-wide work if we popularize it; that is, if we do from the perspective of our own values and interests what our opponents have already done for us, and therefore against us: 'now that we know just how bad criticism's "popularization" might look in hands not our own, we have all the more reason to get busy' (163). Get busy doing what? That is the next question (really the same question all over again), and here Bérubé's answer is a familiar one: get busy translating the languages of academic criticism for non-academic readers (165). But why should these non-academic readers be interested in the languages of academic criticism, either translated or untranslated? Here the answer is clear but finally self-defeating: they are *already* interested:

Is gender performativity something concocted in an academic laboratory, or is it something you can see in *Paris Is Burning*—or down the street? . . . Is it discourse-besotted metahistorians or campaign managers who know that representations are social facts? Do we have to introduce publishers, futures traders and real estate agents to the idea that there's no such thing as 'intrinsic' merit, that merit is a social phenomenon? . . . I don't think so. I think, to put it plain, that all these constituencies are doing the stuff we talk about in a different voice. (166)

But if this is so (and that it is so is, after all, the *thesis* of cultural studies), then it follows that these constituencies don't need our help; and, more importantly, there is no reason for them to help *us* even though we may be the theorists of their activity. Just because we talk about what they do doesn't mean that they will want to promote our talk or even that they will agree with it when they hear it. After all, they don't do what they do because they read Stuart Hall or Judith Butler or Dick Hebdige, and it is quite possible, and even likely, that were they to be told about gender performativity and the social construction of merit, they would reject these notions even if in their own lives they were acting them out.

Only academics, invested as they are in some version of idealism, think that because they have come up with an elegant account of what non-academics are doing those same non-academics will be moved, in admiration, to join forces with the academy. What is missing in this exclusively abstract scenario is what is usually missing: any awareness of the routes and networks that would have to be in place before academic views, however packaged and however translated (and they would have to be), could even have a chance of being heard in extra-academic precincts; what is missing, in Bérubé's own words, is any consideration of 'the social or political conditions under which academic cultural criticism might reach a significant non-academic audience from whom the time, inclination and resources for cultural criticism are never guaranteed, usually unavailable, and only occasionally desirable' (172). Although Bérubé declares that the discussion of these matters is a 'necessity', the discussion never occurs in his text, which continues to issue exhortations—'Profession, revise thyself' (172)—without providing any directions. At the one point where there is a direction—we should lobby 'for tax initiatives . . . to make state taxes more progressive, and education funding less dependent on lotteries and property taxes' (237)—it is obviously a direction we can follow, or attempt to follow, independently of whether or not we have been persuaded by the arguments of cultural studies or have even been exposed to them. What Bérubé never seems to realize is that although, as he puts it, 'the "textual" or the "discursive" is . . . a crucial site of social contestation' (264), the people who *study* that site are not crucial players in the contest.

For a moment, in the closing pages of his book, Bérubé seems close to seeing this as he retreats from his larger claims and imagines a relatively humble role for academic literary work. 'The work of literary critics', he acknowledges, 'just is the work of interpretation, and the teaching and training of literary critics is the teaching of and training in varieties and possibilities of interpretation' (263). This is so reasonable and mild that we might think we were hearing the voice of Frank Kermode when he describes our task as creating readers 'who will want to join us as people who speak with the past and know something of reading as an art to be mastered' and rejects as 'immodest' the notion that by teaching such persons to read 'we are improving them, ethically or civilly' (*An Appetite for Poetry*, Cambridge, Mass., 1989, 58, 56). But immodesty, along with the hope and the claim, immediately returns when Bérubé lists the rewards awaiting those who enrol in his classes:

We make the promise that if you do these things, if you practice the fine arts of textual interpretation, you will 'get more out of' your readings, in terms of your own symbolic economy: you will learn the process of constructing analogies, drawing inferences, making finer and firmer intertextual connections among the texts you've read, and the texts that compose your world. (263)

Up until that last clause this is a thoroughly conventional, even Keatsian–Arnoldian, celebration of the aesthetic sensibility and its pleasures; but with 'and the texts that compose your world' another 'promise' is made, at least implicitly: the promise that if you learn to read in the appropriate manner and teach that way of reading to others, you and they will read the text of the world differently and thereby produce a different, and better, world. (Not only will 'cultural studies . . . make you good', but it will make the world good too.) It is no surprise when the ills of that same world are attributed to the 'bad' reading habits of those who write for and read the wrong journals: 'while we academic readers have been devising more and more exacting ways of reading our texts, our worlds and our critics, the reading skills and reasoning facilities of the *Partisan Review* regulars . . . have become a cause for national alarm' (265). In other words, if only these guys would sit in my classes, and read my writings and the writings of my friends, they would become better thinkers and superior citizens.

The hubris of this is only underscored by the irony that the people Bérubé regularly dismisses and stigmatizes—Dinesh D'Souza, Roger Kimball, Hilton Kramer, Pat Buchanan, William Buckley, etc.—are in fact the public intellectuals he would have us all become. They already command a general audience, write op-ed pieces for major newspapers, appear on C-Span and PBS, and get quoted by congressmen, and, most importantly, those who read them expect them to pronounce on any and all subjects. They are not, however, academics; nor are Michael Kingsley, Paul Berman, Christopher Hitchens, Bill Moyers, Hodding Carter, Frank Rich, David Broder, Edwin Yoder—public intellectuals more in tune with Bérubé's political and social views but no more committed to academic ways of reading than their conservative counterparts. It is not impossible for someone to be an academic *and* a public intellectual—Gary Wills is the best example and he may soon be joined by Henry Louis Gates—it is just that the academic who goes public successfully will have done so not by extending his professional literary skills, but by learning the skills of another profession. If 'public intellectual' is anything, it is a job description, and, as I have already said, it is not a job for which academics, *as* academics, are particularly qualified.

Which returns us to the question of justification. If academics are unsuited, both by inclination and training, for the role of public intellectual, and if access to that role is usually gained by routes not open to most academics (unless they happen to inherit a radio station), and if those who now occupy that role are either hostile or indifferent to academic practices, and if academic

practices are regularly under attack and therefore in need of artic-
ulate and well-positioned defenders, what are we to do?

I can think of two possible strategies, one more likely of success than the other. The less likely would be to persuade college
and university presidents once again to speak out often and force-
fully on national issues and thereby acquire the visibility that
would make them the natural interpreters to the public of the
enterprise whose leadership they have assumed. They would
have no access problem, since, by virtue of the offices they
already hold, whatever they say is newsworthy; it would just be a
matter of seizing the opportunity inherent in their position
rather than running away from it.

But a survey of the present scene suggests that it will be a long
time before any administrators of that resolve and temperament
appear, and, while we wait, I suggest that we try plan two: hire
lobbyists. I don't mean the damage-control types found in most
university public relations offices, who are even more timid than
their bosses and spend much of their time keeping things *out* of
the news or assuring the community that so and so really didn't
mean anything by what he said, and, anyway, he is speaking as a
private citizen, and, besides, he is protected under the doctrine of
academic freedom. No, I mean publicity-seeking types who are
always thinking of ways to grab huge hunks of newspaper space
or air time and fill it with celebrations of the university so compelling that millions of Americans will go to bed thankful that the
members of the Duke English Department are assuring the sur-
vival and improvement of Western civilization. Maybe every
department should have one, a twenty-four-hour-a-day pro-
moter who lets no opportunity go begging and allows no accu-
sation to go unanswered. The Modern Language Association has
gone down this road a little, but more is required. The public
justification of academic practices is too important a task to be
left to academics; for after all—and this has been my message
from the beginning—when there's a job to be done, and you
want it done correctly, call in a professional.

===

The Folger Papers

ON 30 November and 1 December 1990, I gave a workshop at the Folger Library (Washington), in the course of which I first attempted to think through many of the issues discussed in these lectures. As a way of preparing for the seminar, I developed a series of numbered paragraphs on key questions and invited the seminar members to respond to them. As readers will see, much of *Professional Correctness* is the Folger Papers writ large.

1. The Argument for Intention

1. One cannot construe sense without assigning intention; without, that is, assuming that what one is construing issues from a being informed by purposes.

2. Therefore trying to figure out what something means always involves the determination of intention.

3. Therefore there can be no distinction between intentional interpretation and other kinds; all kinds of interpretation are intentional, although that fact says nothing about the nature of the intending agent, the evidence one might consult, the procedures one might follow. *Intentionalism is not an interpretive method, but a fact about interpretation, and one asserted at so general a level that it leaves all empirical interpretive questions (the only kind) open.*

4. It is certainly possible to look for patterns in a text or body of texts independently of intention, but that merely shows that there are things you can do with texts besides interpreting them.

5. Intentionalism is not an issue; it is not a theoretically interesting question because the only question is in what places will you look for evidence of it, and that question is not a theoretical one.

6. Points 1–5 in no way reinstitute the notion of authorial control as exercised by a coherent self that knows its projects unproblematically. Determinations of intention can always be challenged and dislodged, but what will dislodge them will be *other* determinations of intention, and this holds even when the intention you are reading (or rereading) is your own.

2. The Argument against Historicism
(not against history, for that makes no sense)

1. All actions, physical and verbal, are produced in relation to historical circumstances, and it is from those circumstances and not from any eternal or transcendental structures that they receive their meaning.

2. Given that all actions are historically embedded, there can be no ranking of actions (methods, procedures) on a scale of historicity. That is, if everything is historical, methods or approaches cannot be preferred because they are more historical than their rivals. Being historical is not an option, but an inevitability, and therefore historicity cannot be the basis of distinguishing between interpretive styles.

3. What are opposed, then, in debates about method, are versions of historicism; the opposition cannot be between historicism and something else because there is no something else.

4. Debates about method can be adjudicated in relation to any number of standards (all of them interpretive), but the one standard that will not be in play will be the standard of 'more historical' versus 'less historical'.

5. Historicism is itself not a method, and therefore there is no meaning to calling yourself a historicist; it gives you no advan-

APPENDIX: THE FOLGER PAPERS

tage—it doesn't make you more historical than you were before
(what could that possibly mean?)—and those who declare themselves anti-historicist (equally meaningless) suffer no disadvan-
tage by virtue of their theoretical mistake; they are still as
historically embedded as anyone else.

6. It follows then that there can be no methodological consequence of being aware of your embeddedness in history. The
only way that awareness could make a methodological difference
is if it were held to extricate or distance one from the historicity
it announces. But this would be to make the historicist insight
into a way of escaping history, of escaping (by providing a check
on) the local conditions in which one lives and moves and has
one's being. Gadamer says that 'true historical thinking must
take account of its own historicality'; but this is precisely what
true historical thinking (the thinking everyone inevitably
engages in) cannot do without ceasing to be historical, without
offering itself as a vantage-point from which the pressures of the
present historical moment can be surveyed, resisted, and, in a
sense, transcended. In its strong form, the form in which it claims
historical awareness at a level unavailable to those of another
party, the form in which it claims a political superiority based on
superior self-consciousness, the new historicism is the new transcendence.

7. Points 1–6 apply equally well and in the same way to the argument for political criticism and for interdisciplinarity.

3. The Argument against Political Criticism
(not against politics, for that makes no sense)

1. Political criticism is usually understood in one of two ways,
either as the opposite of a criticism that holds itself aloof from the
social and political world—a 'timeless' criticism—or as a criticism whose *intention* is to effect changes in the world beyond the
confines of disciplinary and institutional spaces. Many who call

[129]

difference ?

for, or think they practise, political criticism understand themselves to be doing both these things—opposing timeless criticism and intervening in the world at large—and believe that by doing the first they have already begun to do the second. *criticism that purports to be timeless*

2. The trouble with defining yourself against a timeless criticism, however, is that by the very assumption underlying political criticism—the assumption that all actions are political, conceivable, and 'doable' only within some angled and partisan vision—there can be no such thing as a timeless criticism. If there were such a thing—a criticism in touch with the general truths that underlie the world's appearances—we would all run to it, for in attaching ourselves to it, we would be attaching ourselves to the voice of God.

What is usually called 'timeless' criticism is criticism performed with reference to aesthetic or theological or psychological vocabularies, vocabularies that are of course as historical and political as any other in that they emerge at particular times and under the pressure of certain visions, but vocabularies whose historical and political identity is bound up with the claim to be neither historical nor political. That claim, however, is not a possible one, and when you oppose the work done under its aegis you oppose not the timeless but a version of the timely and you oppose it with, and in the service of, your own version. In short, the clash will always be between two kinds of political criticism, one (falsely) claiming that it is not political, the other (falsely) claiming that only it is political. Nor is it the case, as it is sometimes said, that those who practise 'timeless' criticism are complicit with the forces of the status quo; for, as Dollimore observes, 'it is crucial to realise how essentialist theories of subjectivity have been put to radical use' (*Radical Tragedy*, 2nd edn., New York, 1989, pp. lx–lxii); the reverse is also true; strongly anti-essentialist theories—theories that argue for the unavailability of a transcontextual point of reference—have also been put to conservative use.

3. The upshot then is that there is no such thing as political criticism if you mean by that a criticism that is more (as opposed to

differently) implicated in social, economic, and political phe-nomena than others. Nevertheless, the term 'political criticism' does have an operational force when it is used to identify a par-ticular kind of *literary* activity in which the materials of analysis are political rather than aesthetic or theological or psychological. That of course is an older sense of political criticism. There is a newer sense in which political criticism involves the uncovering of the discursive practices that are constitutive of both the liter-ary work and the culture of which it is an extension. In this exer-cise the line between the literary and the non-literary is blurred and transgressed (and in some cases declared not to exist), and the focus of attention is no longer on features (of tone, style, dic-tion, point of view, voice, etc.) thought of as 'aesthetic', but on cultural patterns that play out in every aspect of social and polit-ical life. To this new work one can put at least two questions: (*a*) is this new work literary criticism or something else, e.g. cultural criticism? and (*b*) if it is cultural criticism (as many would affirm), is it political in the strong sense of intervening actively in the *present* cultural scene? Often these questions are answered within the assumption that the passage from literary criticism (con-ceived of as a discipline-specific activity) to cultural criticism is a passage from something small and artificially isolated to some-thing larger and more inclusive. I would suggest, however, that the passage is one from one disciplinary focus to another, with neither more or less artificial nor more or less inside the confines of the academy. To be sure the two kinds of work are *different*, but the difference is between different forms of academic work, and not between academic work and work that impacts directly on the world beyond the academy.

4. In order for work to impact directly on the world beyond the academy, it must be performed for extra-academic reasons, e.g. to redistribute income, or increase social services, or alter foreign policy; but work done for those reasons would not be recognizably academic, for the evidence it marshalled, the audiences to whom

Is content overlap? (see 139)

that evidence was presented, the forms of argument that were the content of the presentation, and the traditions from which evidence and arguments were drawn would all belong to another context, to another discursive (and material) world. In the academic world, work is by and large *interpretive*, a matter of asking of some text or cultural pattern or historical occurrence 'What does it mean?' or 'What is it about?' or 'What does it manifest?' or 'What does it presage?', questions that are themselves importantly different, but questions that have as their shared aim the getting at the *truth* about something. Such work is political in the sense that whatever form it takes will always occupy a partisan (i.e. contestable and contesting) position within the discursive field of the discipline and its history, but it will not be political in the sense of being answerable (at the moment of its production) to the political urgencies of foreign policy or social welfare or economic crisis. To be sure, academic work, even the work of literary interpretation, can always be put to 'real world' political uses, but when it is, it will no longer be responsible to academic requirements and desiderata; rather it will be employed and evaluated with reference to the requirements and desiderata of some frankly political goal. If, for example, you were to enlist *Paradise Lost* in the service of some political agenda, you would not be asking 'What does it mean?', but 'How can I use one or more answers to the question "What does it mean?" to further this or that purpose?, and your commitment would not be to the rightness of your interpretation but to its effectiveness in achieving your purpose. Not that interpretive work has no purposeful or perlocutionary component, for in performing it you are always trying to persuade someone that you've got it right, but in the context of *that* purpose, you do not have your eye on the political hay that might be made of the interpretation you produce. (This of course would not be true of disciplines which, unlike literary or cultural studies, are so situated as to be immediately in contact with governmental and even global tasks; economists, for example, work within the expectation that what they do will

[132]

influence monetary policy as well as provide solutions to long-standing problems in their discipline; more about this later.) There is a great difference, finally, between trying to figure out what a poem means and trying to figure out which interpretation of it will contribute to the toppling of patriarchy or the subversion of capitalism; the first effort is intelligible within the definitions, specifications, and assumed goals of a discipline and will be so evaluated; the second effort dispenses with or treats with a pragmatic indifference those same definitions, specifications, and goals and aims for something else altogether; and given the present situation of literary studies with respect to issues of national policy (with the *possible* exception of educational policy), the second aims for what it is unlikely to achieve; if you want to do political work, in the 'real world' sense, there are (or should be) better tools in your kit than readings of poems or cultural texts or even cultures.

5. This is where choice comes in. You can choose to do interpretive work, to try and get at the truth about texts or events or cultures (although, as Walter Michaels observes, you can't choose your interpretations), or you can choose to do political work; but you can't do interpretive work (at least not in the humanities) with the intention of doing political work because once you decide to do political work—that is, have before you *from the start* a particular political purpose you are trying to effect—you will be responsive and responsible to criteria that do not respect or even recognize the criteria of the academy. In doing so you will not be dishonest—engaging in questionable scholarly practices—but *differently* honest—not engaging in scholarly practices at all—and that difference, which is procedural, evaluative, and conceptual, makes all the difference.

6. This does not mean, however, that interpretive work has no political implications or consequences. Indeed that would be impossible since, as many have argued, no activity enables or

[133]

authorizes itself, but is given its place *and* its intelligibility by the assumptions, emphases, and relays of power already in place in a society. Thus, as Montrose points out, not only is intellectual work 'socially produced', it is 'also . . . socially productive' ('Professing the Renaissance', in H. Aram Veeser, ed., *The New Historicism*, New York, 1989, 23), looping back to impact upon the discursive/political structures that produced it. Nevertheless, one cannot conclude, as Montrose does, that 'the politics of the academy extend beyond what we casually refer to as "academic politics"' (30); that is, we cannot so conclude if Montrose means that by engaging in the politics of the academy—by proffering this interpretation rather than that (neither of which will have been *chosen*)—we intervene directly, or even in a way that can be calculated, in the politics of our society. Since no action performed in any sphere is without causes or effects in a world of interrelated practices, one's interpretive efforts will in some attenuated, deferred way play into the larger history of the world; but such consequences, while they are real, are not what the academically situated actor has in mind when he or she acts, for his or her mind will at the moment of acting be furnished with criteria and desiderata specific to that situation. Montrose may wish to believe that 'by choosing [exactly the wrong word] to foreground in [his] reading of Shakespeare or Spenser such issues as the politics of gender, the contestation of social constraints' he is 'not only engaged in our . . . continuous re-invention of Elizabethan culture but . . . also endeavoring to make that engagement participate in the re-formation of our own' (30), but unless he thinks of that endeavour as an uncertain and unpredictable by-product (rather than as a strong secondary or even tertiary effect) he is doomed to disappointment. This is not because there could not possibly be a more immediate connection between acts of cultural criticism and outcomes in the larger political world (witness the case of Salman Rushdie or Vaclav Havel), but because given the current distance of cultural criticism from the relays of power (except if you happen to be the

Secretary of Education or the head of the National Endowment for the Humanities or the President of Harvard) such acts will reach a political destination only in the most etiolated fashion.

Of course if you want to hang your hopes on the undoubted fact that the education of the young will finally have consequences for the development of society, and argue that the introduction of gender and other perspectives will influence that development, you will get no argument from me (or probably from any one else), as long as you remember that such consequences are not what you aim at when you do your intellectual work (because if you were aiming at them it would no longer be intellectual work you were doing) and that the way in which the introduction of gender and other perspectives will play out in the lives and careers of our students is entirely contingent.

7. In summary: Either the argument for political criticism is (a) superfluous because all criticism is political in a weak and undistinguishing sense, or (b) it is a call for a certain kind of *academic* work rather than another, or (c) it is a call for a criticism not rooted in the traditions and desiderata of a specific location (the university, the discipline), for a criticism whose concerns and effects are *general rather than local.* If it is the third thing that is meant then it is particularly ironic to find a militant historicism demanding acts that break through or transcend the specific historical occasion of their production, demanding, that is, acts that are timeless.

4. The Argument against Interdisciplinarity
(not against interdisciplinary work, for that makes no sense)

1. The demand for a political criticism is allied with, if not coextensive with, the attack on disciplines, departments, and professions as hegemonic impositions of special and partial perspectives on what should be the field of authentic—i.e. interdisciplinary—knowledge. The reasoning is simple: so long as one's efforts are 'merely' disciplinary—responsible to this or that tradition of academic

inquiry—one will be unable to intervene in the larger political world; therefore one must refuse to be confined within the discipline's assumptions and goals and one must 'break out'. What one breaks out to in some versions of this argument is the general wisdom that lies beyond disciplines, a wisdom that can be received by the general public if it no longer comes packaged in the jargon of the academy: 'Discourse must embody public comprehensibility; that is . . . eschew narrow subservience to disciplines, with their highly differentiated argot' (Ben Agger, *The Decline of Discourse*, New York, 1990, 37). The trouble with disciplines, the same author goes on to say, is that 'work is so highly processed through the editorial and publishing gatekeeping systems that it inevitably takes on a certain homogeneity . . . In academic writing discipline is the real author' (145). The two points are contradictory: on the one hand disciplines are so differentiating that they cut one off from a general perspective; on the other they operate with such constraining force that they suppress difference. The confusion is obvious but helpful, since it allows us to focus on the crucial issue in interdisciplinary studies: the issue of difference. It is in the name of difference—of the recognition of perspectives, materials, and interests excluded from the disciplinary focus—that one calls for interdisciplinary work, for work that insists on looking into the other fellow's back yard; but when the call for interdisciplinary work takes on a political, and usually utopian, cast, difference becomes something to be transcended at that happy moment when all partial and distorting views will be exchanged for the larger and inclusive view of a general wisdom. As Julie Klein puts it, behind the interdisciplinary impulse are 'the ideas of a unified science, general knowledge, synthesis, and the integration of knowledge' (*Interdisciplinarity*, Detroit, 1989, 19).

2. On a less grand scale, the ideas of synthesis and general knowledge have been important to the interdisciplinary ideal as it appears in literary studies. An early but pertinent example is Cleanth Brooks's statement in the last of his exchanges with

Douglas Bush: 'the literary historian and the critic need to work together and . . . the ideal case is that in which both functions are united in one and the same man' ('Marvell's "Horatian Ode"' in W. R. Keast, ed., *Seventeenth Century English Poetry*, London, 1962, 355). In this assertion, one spies the two faces of interdisciplinary transcendence. If one shines the multiple spotlights of diverse disciplines on the poetic object—itself more complex and comprehensive in its essence than any one vocabulary or system of description—it will be truly, that is in a non-angled, non-partial way, seen; and if those same multiple spotlights are turned on in a single brain, that brain and the person it animates will be similarly non-angled, unconfined to any one perspective or methodology. Brooks's 'ideal case' is doubly ideal: it marks the emergence of the ideal (whole, synthesized) object and of the ideal (whole, synthesized) person.

3. The counter-argument is very simple and involves the taking of difference seriously rather than as a regrettable and temporary situation. It goes this way: objects, including texts, do not have an identity apart from some discursive practice, and persons do not have an integrated essence that will emerge if they will only break free of disciplinary constraints. Objects, including texts, come into view *within* the vocabularies of specific enterprises (law, literature, economics, history, etc.) and in relation to the *purposes* of which that enterprise is the instantiation. The application of the vocabularies of different enterprises to an object will not bring out facets of the object's 'complexity' or ineffable thingness, but rather will constitute different objects. One begins with a 'sense of task' derived from some enterprise, some recognizable project, and within that sense one makes use of the materials that come to hand, including materials generated by other enterprises, but materials that will be received (and perceived) in the form appropriate to the job or work you are now doing. Those who complain, as many frequently do, that the materials of their discipline have been 'distorted' or 'trivialized' or 'made into a metaphor' by workers in some

[137]

other discipline are both right and wrong: from the perspective they occupy, the relevance of the materials has been slighted; but those who are looking around for help see the materials as relevant to quite another set of purposes and therefore do not see *them* at all. When Paul de Man and others borrowed the performative–constative distinction from speech act theory, they put it to uses at odds with that theory's basic insight; but since they were not in the speech act business, but in a business where a piece of the speech act vocabulary proved helpful, they are not culpable. Indeed they would only be culpable if all vocabularies were participating in, and therefore responsible to, a single universal task; but vocabularies are specific to and constitutive of particular tasks and acquire whatever force and usefulness they have in relation to specific purposes. The composite historian-critic Brooks imagines would not be a single man but two men, or one (physically defined) man who took on alternate tasks and was, as he moved from one to another, alternate persons. As one person he would see the centrality of X and the appeal of Y; as another X and Y would never come into view, or if they come into view, they would be beside his present point.

The ideals of the unified task, the unified object, the body of unified knowledge, and the unified self all fall together before the fact of irreducible difference. If one is (as everyone now says) always situated, then one's sense of alternative courses of action and of oneself as an actor are situation-specific and can never be made larger although they will often be different.

4. All this has recently been well said by Patrick Hogan:

we should begin by recalling that obligations are to a considerable degree related to functions or descriptions. Thus as someone teaching *King Lear*—that is, insofar as I am operating under the description 'teacher of *King Lear*'—I am obligated to seek in class to make *King Lear* comprehensible to my students, to meet with these students outside of class in order to help them understand *King Lear*, and so on. My obligations as a human being in general do not obligate me to make *King Lear* comprehensible. It is only my obligations as an instructor that do so. (*The Politics of Interpretation*, New York, 1990, 184)

[138]

I would go further: there are no 'obligations as a human being in general', only those obligations that seem obvious and compelling given some particular function or role. This includes the role of the so-called general or public intellectual whose supposed disappearance has been lamented by both the left and the right (see Agger, Jacoby, A. Bloom, Bruce Robbins, Page Smith, John Silber, Robert Alter, Frank Kermode, etc.). The public intellectual is merely someone situated not in a university but in some other institutional space, the coffee-house in eighteenth-century England and 1960s Berkeley, Broadway and 116th Street in the 1930s, 1940s, and 1950s, Cambridge and Concord, Massachusetts, when our literary republic was young, and so on. In whatever forum he or she appears, the public intellectual has a task as specific as the task of a specialist in medieval metrics, and his or her audience is no less specialized, even if it is (at least potentially) larger. 'Public intellectual' is a *job description* not an honorific title awarded only to those who have escaped the confines of all jobs, and it is a job description that will have different requirements and display different (but always special and limited) practices at different times. At present it seems to be a job description for talk show hosts which will seem either a good or bad thing in so far as you like or dislike Phil Donahue, Ted Koppel, Dick Cavett, Pat Buchanan, William Buckley, Bill Moyers, and (once upon a time) John Searle. In short, the public intellectual is another professional, practising another discipline and enacting a vision no more or less grand than the vision of any other professional in any other discipline. The gospel of interdisciplinarity depends on the possibility of performing acts that are more than locally intelligible and therefore more than locally consequential. There are no such acts, although, given certain political conditions, acts proceeding from some local perspective can command the field. This, however, will not be the triumph of interdisciplinarity, but the triumph of one discipline or angled project over all others.

5. Disciplines are conservative, which means no more than that the sense of purpose at their core will sustain itself usually by

taking into itself and making its own the challenges history and chance provide. It should come as no surprise then to find that the energies generated in the effort to undo disciplines, and by undoing them to transform academic work into work that is truly political (that is, truly interdisciplinary), are continually being absorbed and domesticated by their supposed object. As Don Wayne puts it (*Shakespeare Reproduced*, New York, 1987, 61) there is a danger that the new focus on 'intertextual relations . . . will operate in our criticism in the way that generic categories, narrative functions and stylistic devices did formerly', that is, as discipline-specific constructs that call us to more disciplinary work. Michael Bristol sadly predicts that 'critical scholarship is likely to result in legitimation rather than in practically effective critique' (220). He is right, if by 'effective critique' he means a critique of the world outside the academy rather than (the words are again Wayne's) 'just the disestablishment of an existing critical orthodoxy' (62) by a new orthodoxy.

6. In the end, the desire for a truly historical criticism, for a truly political criticism, and a truly interdisciplinary criticism is the familiar desire of the academic, and especially of the humanist academic, to be something other than what he or she is. It can't be that producing a new account of *King Lear* for our peers is all we can do; it must be that if we get the right account—that is, the account sufficiently responsive to the society's larger needs—the society will hearken to us, and our parents will finally understand why we made this apparently quixotic career choice. Thirty years ago we could have presented ourselves to ourselves and to others as the guardians of a cultural heritage (and some of course ardently wish that we once again do so) or as, if not the unacknowledged legislators of the world, at least the necessary vehicles of these legislators ('make me thy lyre'). Those justifications, however, have been largely discredited and as a result many have turned to new justifications, different to be sure from the old but alike in claiming for our labours effects beyond the classroom and even beyond the stars. Justifications, however, are never available

from the outside. If you ask, as do many of us, what good are we from the perspective of those who wish to cure cancer or bring peace to the Middle East, the answer can only be disheartening; but if, in response to the demand for justification, we tell ourselves and others the story of our discipline, and immerse ourselves, as we were immersed in graduate school, in the lore and skill of a specialized craft, we may find a satisfaction in that story, and if we really learn how to live with ourselves and not for a self we dream of becoming, we may even find satisfaction in our satisfaction. When all is said and done, there is no reason for any discipline or enterprise to exist except for what is brought into the world by the possibility of its practice. What you gain by maintaining an enterprise is the very special and specific pleasures and consolations it affords. Those pleasures and consolations should be thought of neither as the vehicles of our salvation nor as obstacles to it; they are what they are and so are we.

Index

[143]

INDEX

INDEX

INDEX